WORLD DEVOTIONAL CLASSICS

GENERAL EDITOR: THOMAS S. KEPLER

The Private Devotions of
Lancelot Andrewes

THE PRIVATE
DEVOTIONS OF
Lancelot Andrewes

EDITED AND WITH AN INTRODUCTION BY

THOMAS S. KEPLER

PH.D., S.T.D., D.D.

GRADUATE SCHOOL OF THEOLOGY

OBERLIN COLLEGE

Cleveland *New York*

THE WORLD PUBLISHING COMPANY

Library of Congress Catalog Card Number: 56–9258

FIRST EDITION

BV
4830
,A6513
1956

WP756

COPYRIGHT © 1956 BY THE WORLD PUBLISHING COMPANY
MANUFACTURED IN THE UNITED STATES OF AMERICA

Contents

Morning Prayers

Evening Prayers

Confessional Prayers

Prayers of Deprecation

Prayers of Penitence

Prayers of Thanksgiving

Prayers for Holy Communion

Introduction

IN THE GAMUT of devotional literature one can find no deeper spiritual message than that uttered in Bishop Lancelot Andrewes' *Private Devotions:* "Like the Confessions of Saint Augustine, like many of the Psalms, the *Preces privatae* unlock the doors of a sanctuary where a saint kneels in fellowship with God." [1] "It may be truly said of him [Lancelot Andrewes] as it was said of another, that the very dust of his writings is gold."

Four quotations from the earliest biographer of Lancelot Andrewes give us insight into the life of this man who left his spiritual autobiography to posterity. In 1650 Henry Isaacson wrote: "What he [Lancelot Andrewes] did, when he was a child, and a schoolboy, is not now known, but he hath been sometimes heard to say, that when he was a young scholar in the University, and so all his time onward, he never loved or used any games or ordinary recreations, either within doors, as cards, dice, tables, chess, or the like; or abroad, as

[1] H. B. Swete, *The Devotions of Bishop Andrewes* (New York: The Macmillan Co., 1920), p. x.

buts, quoits, bowls, or any such: but his ordinary exercise and recreation was walking either alone by himself, or with some other selected companion, with whom he might confer and argue, and recount their studies; and he would often profess that to observe the grass, herbs, corn, trees, cattle, earth, waters, heavens, any of the creatures, and to contemplate their natures, orders, qualities, virtues, uses, etc., was ever to him the greatest mirth, content, and recreation that could be: and this he held to his dying day. . . .

"His first and principal virtue was his singular zeal and piety, which showed itself, not only in his private and secret devotions between God and himself, in which, they that were about him well perceived that he daily spent many hours, yea, and the greatest part of his life in holy prayers, and abundant tears, the signs whereof they often discovered,—but also wherein he behaved himself so humbly, devoutly, and reverently, that it could not but move others to follow his example. . . .

"After dinner, for two or three hours space, he would willingly pass the time, either in discourse with his guests or other friends, or in despatch of his own temporal affairs, or of those, who, by reason of his Episcopal jurisdiction, attended him; and being quit of these and the like occasions, he would return to his study, where he spent the afternoon even till bed-time, except some friend

took him off to supper, and then did he eat but
sparingly. . . .

"Now let us lay all these together: his zeal and
piety; his charity and compassion; his fidelity and
integrity; his gratitude and thankfulness; his
munificence and bounty; hospitality, humanity,
affability, and modesty; and to these, his inde-
fatigability in study, and the fruits of his labours
in his sermons and writings, together with his
profundity of learning; his wit, memory, judgment, gravity, and humility. His detestation of all
vices and sin, but especially of three (usury,
simony, sacrilege). All which, by couching them
only in this compend, we have seen in him, as *ex
ungue leonem*, or by Hercules' foot his whole
body; and consider whether the Church of God
in general, and this in particular, did not suffer
an irreparable loss by his death."[2]

Lancelot Andrewes held fame in many realms:
(1) One of the rarest linguists in Christendom, he
knew fifteen languages. Oddly, he could write
with better literary style in either Greek or Latin
than in English. (2) Many called him the out-
standing preacher of his day, although this com-
pliment was questioned by some. A Presbyterian
Lord said of him after his sermon in Edinburgh
Chapel, "No doubt your Majesty's bishop is a
learned man, but he cannot preach. He rather

[2] Henry Isaacson *Life and Death of Lancelot
Andrewes* (1650).

plays with his text than preaches it." (3) He was
one of the translators of the King James Version
of the Bible, being on the commission responsible
for the books from Genesis through Second
Kings. (4) He was a favorite of King James I and
other leaders of the English government. He held
the bishopric at Chichester, Ely, and Winchester.
It was not an office easy to handle during the time
of James I when the bench of bishops was com-
posed of servile and shortsighted men. Says one
critic of Bishop Andrewes during this regime, "I
feel pity for him—for no man could retain integrity amidst such a group—compromised, cor-
rupted, demoralised." (5) He was a close friend
of Francis Bacon. Bacon's *Holy War* was dedi-
cated to Andrewes; and Andrewes was asked to
criticize Bacon's *The Advancement of Learning*
and other writings. When Lord Chancellor
Bacon was on trial for bribery, it was Bishop
Andrewes who heard his confession and submission, only sorrowful that earlier he had not acted
more as Bacon's intercessor.

All of these events in the life of Lancelot
Andrewes seem minute, however, when com-
pared to his one great gift to the world, his
Private Devotions. "To myself one of the chiefest
compensations and off-sets for the reign of James
the First is this, that the *Private Devotions* of
Lancelot Andrewes were being continually com-
posed and were being continually employed,

were being continually wrung out of him, during the whole course of that so mischievous and insufferable reign." [3]

The characteristic note of *Private Devotions* is repentance. These writings depict the yearning of a frail human spirit for God's overflowing mercy, the desire of an incomplete personality to make himself worthy of God's compassionate love and forgiveness. Cries Lancelot Andrewes, "I need more grief, I plainly need more of it. I am far from that which I ought to have. I can sin much! I cannot repent much. My dryness! My dryness! Woe unto me! Would that I had such grief, or even more! But of myself I cannot obtain it. I am parched, I am parched like a potsherd. Woe is me! Thou, O Lord, O Lord, a fountain of tears. Give me a molten heart."

Private Devotions was never written for publication. It was placed in the hands of William Laud, then bishop of Bath and Wells, on Andrewes' deathbed in 1626. Not until 1675, thirty years after Laud's death, was the first nearly complete edition in the English language published by the Oxford Press. *Private Devotions* was originally written in two volumes for Lancelot Andrewes' personal use, the first volume in Greek and well planned, the second volume in

---

[3] Alexander Whyte, *Lancelot Andrewes and His Private Devotions* (Edinburgh and London: Oliphant Anderson and Ferrier, 1896), p. 32.

Latin with less careful organization. "Had you seen," wrote Richard Drake, "the original manuscript, happy in the glorious deformity thereof, being slubbered with its author's pious hands and watered with his penitential tears, you would have been forced to confess, that book belonged to no other than to pure and primitive devotion."

For *Private Devotions* Bishop Andrewes borrowed the finest expressions of the Psalms, the Prophets, the Gospels, the Epistles, the Sermons of the Greek and Latin Fathers, the classical liturgies and litanies, and wove them into the fabric of his own soul. A roll call of the writers, besides those of the Bible, whose contributions appear in *Private Devotions*, includes these: *Church Fathers*—Irenaeus, Tertullian, Saint Cyprian, Dion Chrysostom, Saint Jerome, Saint Augustine, the Gregories; *Medieval Writers*—Alcuin, Saint Anselm, Saint Bernard of Clairvaux, Peter Lombard, Saint Thomas Aquinas, Thomas Bradwardine, Gerson; *Sixteenth-Century Writers*—Erasmus, Saint John Fisher; *Classical Writers of Greece and Rome*—Euripides, Aristophanes, Horace, Seneca; *Liturgies and Prayers* from Saint James, Saint Basil, the *Western Hours*, *Missal and Manual*, several of the *Primers*, *Book of Common Prayer*, John Knox's *Book of Common Order*, the Apostles' and Nicene Creeds.

Monotony of style is lacking in *Private Devotions*, even when a similar pattern of worship is

followed for seven successive days of the week.
Nor is any area of the prayer life neglected:
preparation for prayer, morning and evening
prayers, prayers of deprecation, prayers of
thanksgiving, prayers for holy communion, prayers of intercession, prayers of confession are all
included. The heart of the first volume of *Private
Devotions*, a Week of Prayer, is fashioned after
the first chapter of Genesis. In this "week" each
of the seven days opens with adoration of the
work God had performed on that day, and for
each day there are six suggestions for a pattern of
worship: (1) meditation and adoration (introduction), (2) confession of sin, (3) prayer for
grace, (4) confession of faith (profession), (5)
intercession, (6) thanksgiving (praise). The basic
religious purpose in all of these devotional patterns is thus described: "Members of the church
who in the exercise of their discretion abstain
from using the ministry of private confession and
absolution will find no better substitute than these
acts of penitence, with their intimate revelation
of personal sinfulness, and their firm trust in
God's mercy through Christ." [4]

To read the passages of *Private Devotions* with
the spirit of those who "hunger and thirst after
righteousness" will be the surest way to understand their spiritual depth. The worth which the
worshipper can hope to find in these spiritual

[4] Swete, p. xvii.

treasures is well described by two critics, writing a generation apart: Alexander Whyte (in 1896): "We have the Confessions of Augustine, the Prayers and Soliloquies of Anselm, the unfinished Holy Week and other great prayers and praises of Jacob Behmen, the Golden Grove of Jeremy Taylor, the Private Devotions of Lancelot Andrewes. . . . But, for its peculiar purpose and for its special use, Andrewes' *Private Devotions* stands out at the head of them all. There is nothing in the whole range of devotional literature to be set aside Andrewes' incomparable *Devotions*." [5] Lynn Harold Hough (in 1945): "The *Private Devotions* of Bishop Lancelot Andrewes [is] still the supreme devotional classic possessed by the Christian Church. The light of God shines in it. . . . Here you see the humble penitent beating his breast in the presence of the white glory of the Holy God." [6]

This volume of *Private Devotions* is based on Cardinal John Henry Newman's English translation (made in 1845) of Volume One from Greek and John Mason Neale's English translation (made in 1843) of Volume Two from Latin. Instead of retaining the original order in the two volumes of *Private Devotions*, the prayers have

[5] Whyte, p. 31.
[6] Lynn Harold Hough, *The Meaning of Human Experience* (New York and Nashville: Abingdon-Cokesbury Press, 1945), pp. 181, 361.

been rearranged so that those of a similar purpose are together. The biblical references used by Bishop Andrewes are not those of the King James Version, though he was one of its translators.

Important Events in the Life of Lancelot Andrewes

1555	Born in London.
1563	At the Cooper's School.
1565	At the Merchant Tailor's School.
1571	Scholar at Pembroke College, Cambridge.
	Scholar at Jesus College, Oxford.
1574–75	February 4, received B.A.
1576	Fellow of Pembroke Hall.
1578	Received M.A.
1580	Ordained Deacon.
	Junior Treasurer of Pembroke Hall.
1581	Senior Treasurer of Pembroke Hall.
	July 11, incorporated M.A., Oxford.
1585	Received B.D.
1586	Chaplain to Henry Earl of Huntingdon.
	Chaplain to Archbishop Whitgift.
	Chaplain to Queen Elizabeth.
1589	Vicar of St. Giles's, Cripplegate.
	Prebend of Southwell.
	Prebend of St. Paul's.
1590	Master of Pembroke Hall.

1594   D.D. received.
        On commission for inquiring into Ec-
            clesiastical Courts in the Diocese of
            London.
1597   Prebend of Westminster.
1601   Dean of Westminster.
1603   July 25, assisted at King James's Corona-
            tion.
        August 26, on the High Commission.
1603-4 January 14–16, at Hampton Court Con-
            ference where he defended the use of
            the cross at baptism.
1604   July 22, appointed one of the translators
            of the Bible. He and his group were to
            translate the Pentateuch and the books
            of his history from Joshua to First
            Chronicles exclusive.
1605   November 3, consecrated Bishop of
            Chichester by Richard Bancroft
            (Archbishop of Canterbury), Richard
            Vaughan (Bishop of London), John
            Jegon (Bishop of Norwich), Thomas
            Ravis (Bishop of Gloucester), and
            William Barlow (Bishop of Roches-
            ter).
1609   Published *Tortura Torti*.
        July 25, Rector of Cheam.
        September 22, translated to Ely as
            Bishop.

1610   June 4, present at the creation of Henry, Prince of Wales.

1612   December 7, at Prince Henry's funeral.

1613   On a commission to inquire into the validity of the marriage of the Earl of Essex and the Lady Frances Howard.

1614   April 5, attended the King on the opening of Parliament.

1614–15   March, attended the King to Cambridge.

1616   September 29, Privy Councillor of England.

    November 4, present at the creation of Charles, Prince of Wales.

1617   April 5, on a commission for releasing certain persons imprisoned for not taking the oath of allegiance.

    March 15–September 16, attended the King of Scotland.

    Privy Councillor of Scotland.

1617–18   On a commission respecting the tithes of the London Clergy.

1618   June 23, on a commission for banishing Jesuits.

    August 3, translated to Winchester as Bishop.

1618–19   January 1, Dean of Chapel Royal.

1619   March and April, attended the King at Royston during his illness.

May 13, present at funeral of the Queen.

1620   March 26, attended the King to St.
Paul's, to give encouragement to its
repair.

April 27, on a commission for selling
some of the crown jewels.

April 29, on the High Commission.

August 31, entertained the King at Farnham.

September 17, consecrated Jesus Chapel,
near Southampton. His chaplains on
this occasion were Matthew and
Christopher Wren.

1620   March, at the rising of the Convocation
he and Bishop Montaigne of Lincoln,
in the name of the other bishops, pre-
sented to the King at Hampton Court
a grant of the subsidies passed by the
Clergy of the Province of Canterbury.

1621   April 30, attended with other peers on
Lord Bacon, to ascertain from him
whether he acknowledged as his own
the petition and confession made in his
name to the House.

June 10, present at the delivery of the
Great Seal to John Williams, Dean of
Westminster.

October 3, on a commission to inquire

whether Archbishop Abbot had in-
curred any irregularity by casual
homicide.

November 22, on a commission for dis-
pensing with the Archbishop for any
irregularities.

1622   April 20, on a commission for banishing
Jesuits and others.

May 31, joined the Lords of the Council
in an order to the Vice-Chancellor of
Oxford to burn Paraeus' Works.

August 10–15, entertained the King at
Farnham.

1623   July 20, present at the ceremony of the
King swearing to the articles of the
Spanish match.

1624   December 24, on a commission for banishing Jesuits and seminary priests.

1624–25 January 1, on the High Commission. In
consequence of illness, unable to at-
tend King James in his last sickness.

1625   May 9, appears to have resigned his
Almonership before this time, as
Bishop Montaigne of London is now
mentioned as holding this office.

June 7, on a commission for mortgaging
some of the crown lands to Edward
Allen and others.

1625–26   February 15, on the High Commission.
          March 6, on a commission for banishing
             Jesuits.
          March 8, on a commission for reprieve
             of persons condemned to death.

1626   September 25, died at the age of
          seventy-one. Buried in the upper aisle
          of the parish church of St. Saviour's
          in Southwark, where his executors
          erected to him a monument of marble
          and alabaster.

This Chronology is taken from *Library of Anglo-Catholic Theology: Andrewes' Minor Works. Life. Indexes.* "Appendix A." Oxford: John Henry Parker, 1854.

Writings of Lancelot Andrewes

The Private Devotions of
Lancelot Andrewes

Preparation for Prayer

DAILY PRAYERS

Preparation

I. TIMES OF PRAYER

Always. (Luke xviii.1)

Without ceasing. (1 Thess. v.17)

At all times. (Eph. vi.18)

Samuel among such as call upon His name. (Ps. xcix.6)

God forbid that I should sin against the Lord in ceasing to pray for you, and shewing you the good and the right way. (1 Sam. xii.23)

We will give ourselves continually to prayer and to the ministry of the word. (Acts vi.4)

He kneeled upon his knees three times a day, and prayed and gave thanks before his God, as he did aforetime. (Dan. vi.10)

In the evening, and morning, and at noon day will I pray, and that instantly, and He shall hear my voice. (Ps. lv.18)

Seven times a day do I praise Thee. (Ps. cxix.164)

1. In the morning, a great while before day. (Mark i.35)

2. In the morning watch. (Ps. lxiii.6) [see also Ps. cxxx.6.]

3. The third hour of the day. (Acts ii.15)

4. About the sixth hour. (Acts x.9)

5. The hour of prayer, the ninth. (Acts iii.1)

6. The eventide. (Gen. xxiv.63)

7. By night. (Ps. cxxxiv.2)

At midnight. (Ps. cxix.62)

II. PLACES OF PRAYER

In all places where I record My Name, I will come to thee, and I will bless thee. (Exod. xx.24)

Let Thine eyes be open toward this house night and day, even toward the place of which Thou hast said, My Name shall be there; that Thou mayest hearken unto the prayer which Thy servant shall make toward this place.

(1 Kings viii.29)

Thou that hearest the prayer
unto Thee shall all flesh come.
The fierceness of man shall turn to Thy praise,
and the fierceness of them shalt Thou refrain.
As for me, I will come into Thy house
even upon the multitude of Thy mercy,
and in Thy fear will I worship
toward Thy Holy Temple.
Hear the voice of my humble petitions,

when I cry unto Thee;
when I told up my hands
toward the mercy-seat of Thy Holy
Temple.
We wait for Thy loving-kindness,
O God,
in the midst of Thy Temple.

1. Among the faithful and in the congregation. (Ps. cxi.1)

2. Enter into thy closet, and, when thou hast shut thy door, pray to thy Father which is in secret. (Matt. vi.6)

3. They went up into an upper room. (Acts i.13)

4. He went up upon the housetop to pray. (Acts x.9)

5. They went up together into the Temple. (Acts iii.1)

6. We kneeled down on the shore, and prayed. (Acts xxi.5)

7. He went forth over the brook Cedron, where was a garden. (John xviii.1)

8. Let them rejoice in their beds. (Ps. cxlix.5)

9. He departed into a desert place and there prayed. (Mark i.35)

10. In every place lifting up holy hands without wrath and doubting. (1 Tim. ii.8)

III. CIRCUMSTANCES OF PRAYER

1. Kneeling,   *humiliation.*
   He kneeled down and prayed. (Luke xxii.41)
   He went a little further, and fell on His
face, and prayed. (Matt. xxvi.39)
   My soul is brought low, even unto the
                            dust,
      my belly cleaveth unto the ground.
2. Sinking the head,   *shame.*
   Drooping the face, [Ezra. ix.6]
3. Smiting the breast, [Luke xviii.13]
                            indignation.
4. Shuddering, [Acts xvi.29]   *fear.*
5. Groaning, [Isa. lix.11]   *sorrow.*
   Clasping of hands.
6. Raising of eyes and hands, [Ps. xxv.
   15; cxliii.6]   *vehement desire.*
7. Blows, [Ps. lxxiii.14]   *revenge.*

(2 Cor. vii.11)

PREPARATION TO PRAYER

Let my prayer ascend,
come up to Thee, (2 Chron. xxx.27)
enter, (Ps. lxxxviii.2)
appear in Thy presence, (Ps. cxli.2)
find grace,
approach unto Thee; (Ps. cxix.109)
and let it not return unto me void,

but as Thou knowest, and canst, and willest.
Hear, (Ps. cxix.149)
bow down Thine ear, (Ps. lxxxvi.1; Dan. ix.19)
hearken and consider, (Ps. xlv.10; Lam. i.12)
understand,
listen, (Ps. lxiv.1)
hearken and do. (Dan. ix.19)

An Order of Prayers
for the Week

THE FIRST DAY

Introduction

Through the tender mercies of our God
the day-spring from on high hath visited us.
Glory be to Thee, O Lord, glory to Thee.
Creator of the light,
and Enlightener of the world,—
of the visible light,
The Sun's ray, a flame of fire,
day and night,
evening and morning,—
of the light invisible,
the revelation of God,
writings of the Law,
oracles of Prophets,
music of Psalms,
instruction of Proverbs,
experience of Histories,—
light which never sets.
God is the Lord who hath shewed us light;
bind the sacrifice with cords,
yea even unto the horns of the altar.

O by Thy resurrection raise us up
unto newness of life,
supplying to us frames of repentance.
The God of peace,
who did bring again from the dead
the great Shepherd of the sheep,
through the Blood of the everlasting covenant,
our Lord Jesus Christ,
perfect us in every good work,
to do His will,
working in us what is acceptable before Him,
through Jesus Christ,
to whom be glory forever.

Thou who didst send down on Thy disciples
on this day
Thy Thrice-holy Spirit,
withdraw not Thou the gift, O Lord, from us,
but renew it in us, day by day,
who ask Thee for it.

Confession

Merciful and pitiful Lord,
Long-suffering and full of pity,
I have sinned, Lord, I have sinned against Thee;
O me, wretched that I am,
I have sinned, Lord, against Thee
much and grievously,
in attending on vanities and lies.

I conceal nothing:
I make no excuses.
I give Thee glory, O Lord, this day,
I denounce against myself my sins;
truly I have sinned before the Lord,
and thus and thus have I done.
I have sinned and perverted
that which was right,
and it profited me not.
And what shall I now say?
or with what shall I open my mouth?
What shall I answer, seeing I have done it?
Without plea, without defense,
self-condemned, am I.
I have destroyed myself.
Unto Thee, O Lord, belongeth righteousness,
but unto me confusion of face,
because Thou art just in all that is come upon me,
for Thou hast done right,
but I have done wickedly.
And now, Lord, what is my hope?
Truly my hope is even in Thee,
if hope of salvation remain to me,
if Thy loving-kindness cover
the multitude of my iniquities.
O remember, what my substance is,
the work of Thine hands,
the likeness of Thy countenance,
the cost of Thy Blood,
a name from Thy Name,

a sheep of Thy pasture,
a son of the covenant.
Despise not Thou the work of Thine own hands.
Hast Thou made for nought
Thine own image and likeness?
for nought, if Thou destroy it.
And what profit is there in my blood?
Thine enemies will rejoice;
may they never rejoice, O Lord!
Grant not to them my destruction.
Look upon the face of Thine Anointed,
and in the Blood of Thy covenant,
the propitiation for the sins of the whole world,
Lord, be propitious unto me, a sinner;
even unto me, O Lord, of sinners
chief, chiefest and greatest;
for Thy Name's sake be merciful unto my sin,
for it is great: it exceeds.
For Thy Name's sake, that Name,
beside which, none other under heaven
is given among men,
whereby we must be saved,
the Spirit Himself helping our infirmities,
and making intercession for us,
with plaints unutterable.
For the tender yearnings of the Father,
the bloody wounds of the Son,
the unutterable plaints of the Spirit,
give ear, O Lord, have mercy, O Lord,
O Lord, hearken and do;

defer not, for Thine own sake,
O my God.
For me, I forget not my sins,
they are ever before me;
I remember them in the bitterness of my soul;
I am anxious about them;
I turn away and groan,
I have indignation and revenge
and wrath against myself.
I despise and bruise my own self,
that my penitence, Lord, O Lord,
is not deeper, is not fuller;
help Thou mine impenitence.
And more, and still more,
pierce Thou, rend, crush my heart;
and remit, forgive, pardon
what things are grief to me,
and offense of heart.
Cleanse Thou me from secret faults,
and keep Thy servant also from
presumptuous sins.
Magnify Thy mercies toward the
wretched sinner;
and in season, Lord, say to me,
Be of good cheer; thy sins are forgiven thee;
My grace is sufficient for thee.
Say unto my soul, I am thy salvation.
Why art thou so heavy, O my soul?
and why art thou so disquieted within thee?

Return unto thy rest, O my soul,
for the Lord hath rewarded thee.
O Lord, rebuke me not in Thine indignation,
neither chasten me in Thy displeasure.
I said, I will confess my sins unto the Lord,
and so Thou forgavest the wickedness of my sin.
Lord, Thou knowest all my desire,
and my groaning is not hid from Thee.
Have mercy upon me, O God,
after Thy great goodness,
according to the multitude of Thy mercies
do away mine offenses.
Thou shalt arise, and have mercy on me, O Lord,
for it is time that Thou have mercy upon me,
yea, the time is come.
If Thou, O Lord, shouldest mark iniquities,
O Lord, who shall stand?
Enter not into judgment with Thy servant,
O Lord,
for in Thy sight shall no man living be justified.

Prayer for Grace

My hands will I lift up
unto Thy commandments which I have loved.
Open Thou mine eyes that I may see,
incline my heart that I may desire,
order my steps that I may follow,
the way of Thy commandments.

O Lord God, be Thou to me a God,
and beside Thee none else,
none else, nought else with Thee.
Vouchsafe to me, to worship Thee and
serve Thee
1. in truth of spirit;
2. in reverence of body;
3. in blessing of lips;
4. in private and in public;
5. to pay honor to them that have the
rule over me,
by obedience and submission,
to shew affection to my own,
by carefulness and providence;
6. to overcome evil with good;
7. to possess my vessel in sanctification and honor;
8. to have my converse without covetousness,
content with what I have;
9. to speak the truth in love;
10. to be desirous not to lust,
not to lust passionately,
not to go after lusts.

(*The Hedge of the Law, i.e. Precautions*)

1. To bruise the serpent's head. (Gen. iii.15)
2. To remember my latter end. (Deut. xxvii.29)
3. To cut off opportunities. (2 Cor. xi.12)
4. To be sober. (1 Pet. v.8)

5. Not to sit idle. (Matt. xx.6)

6. To shun the wicked. (Ps. xxvi.5)

7. To cleave to the good. (Rom. xii.9)

8. To make covenant with the eyes. (Job xxxi.1)

9. To bring my body into subjection. (1 Cor. ix.27)

10. To give myself unto prayer. (1 Cor. vii.5)

11. To betake myself to penitence. (2 Pet. iii.9)

> Hedge up my way with thorns,
> that I find not the path
>   for following vanity.
> Hold Thou me in with bit and bridle,
> lest I fall from Thee.
> O Lord compel me to come in to Thee.

Profession

> I believe, O Lord,
> in Thee, Father, Word, Spirit, One God;
> that by Thy fatherly love and power
> all things were created;—
> that by Thy goodness and love to man
> all things have been begun anew
>   in Thy Word,—
> Who for us men and for our salvation,
> was made flesh,
> was conceived and born,
> suffered and was crucified,

died and was buried,
descended and rose again,
ascended and sat down,
will return and will repay;—
that by the shining-forth and working
of Thy Holy Spirit,
hath been called out of the whole world
a peculiar people into a polity,
in belief of the truth
and sanctity of living:—
that in it we are partakers
of the communion of saints
and forgiveness of sins
in this world,—
that in it we are waiting
for resurrection of the flesh
and life everlasting
in the world to come.—
This most holy faith
which was once delivered to the saints
I believe, O Lord;
help Thou mine unbelief,
and vouchsafe to me
to love the Father for His fatherly love,
to reverence the Almighty for His power,
as a faithful Creator, to commit my soul to Him
in well doing;
vouchsafe to me to partake
from Jesus of salvation,

from Christ of anointing,
from the Only-begotten of adoption;
to worship the Lord
for His conception in faith,
for His birth in humility,
for His sufferings in patience and hatred of sin;
for His cross to crucify beginnings,
for His death to mortify the flesh,
for His burial to bury evil thoughts in
good works,
for His descent to meditate upon hell,
for His resurrection upon newness of life,
for His ascension, to mind things above,
for His sitting on high, to mind the good
things on His right,
for His return, to fear His second appearance,
for judgment, to judge myself ere I be judged.
From the Spirit
vouchsafe me the breath of salutary grace.
In the Holy Catholic Church
to have my own calling, and holiness, and portion,
and a fellowship
of her sacred rites, and prayers,
fastings and groans,
vigils, tears, and sufferings,
for assurance of remission of sins,
for hope of resurrection and translation
to eternal life.

Intercession

O Hope of all the ends of the earth,
and of them that remain in the broad sea;
O Thou on whom our fathers hoped,
and Thou didst deliver them;
on whom they waited,
and were not confounded;
O my Hope from my youth,
from my mother's breasts;
on whom I have been cast from the womb,
be Thou my Hope
now and evermore,
and my portion in the land of the living:
In Thy nature,
in Thy names, in Thy types,
in word and in deed,
my Hope,
let me not be disappointed of my hope.
O the Hope of all the ends of the earth,
remember Thy whole creation for good,
visit the world in Thy compassion;
O guardian of men,
O loving Lord,
remember all our race.
Thou who hast shut up all in unbelief,
on all have pity, O Lord.
O Thou who didst die and rise again,
to be Lord both of the dead and living,

live we or die we,
Thou art our Lord;
Lord, have pity on living and dead.
O helper of the helpless,
seasonable aid in affliction,
remember all who are in necessity,
and need Thy succor.
O God of grace and truth,
establish all who stand in truth and grace,
restore all who are sick with heresies and sins.
O wholesome defense of Thine Anointed,
remember Thy congregation
which Thou hast purchased and redeemed of old.
O grant to all believers
one heart and one soul.
Thou that walkest amid the golden candlesticks,
remove not our candlestick
out of its place.
Amend what are wanting,
establish what remain,
which Thou art ready to cast away,
which are ready to die.
O Lord of the harvest
send forth laborers, made sufficient by Thee,
into Thy harvest.
O portion of those
who wait in Thy temple,
grant to our clergy,
rightly to divide the word of truth,
rightly to walk in it;

grant to Thy Christian people
to obey and submit to them.
O King of nations, unto the ends
of the earth;
strengthen all the states
of the inhabited world,
as being Thy ordinance,
though a creation of man.
Scatter the nations that delight in war,
make wars to cease in all the earth.
O expectation of the isles and their hope,
Lord, save this island,
and all the country in which we sojourn,
from all affliction, peril, and need.
Lord of lords, Ruler of rulers,
remember all rulers
to whom Thou hast given rule in the earth,
and O remember specially
our divinely-guarded king,
and work with him more and more,
and prosper his way in all things.
Speak good things unto his heart,
for Thy Church, and all Thy people,
grant to him profound and perpetual peace,
that in his tranquillity
we may lead a quiet and peaceable life
in all godliness and honesty.
O Thou by whom are ordained the
powers that be,
grant to those who are chief in court,

to be chief in virtue and Thy fear;
grant to the Parliament Thy holy wisdom;
to our great men, to do nothing against
but for the truth;
to the courts of law, Thy judgments,
to judge in all things concerning all
without preference, without partiality.
O God of armies,
give a prosperous course and strength
to all the Christian army,
against the enemies of our most holy faith.
Grant to our population
to be subject unto the higher powers,
not only for wrath, but also for conscience' sake.
Grant to farmers and graziers good seasons;
to the fleet and fishers fair weather;
to tradesmen, not to overreach one another;
to mechanics, to pursue their business lawfully,
down to the meanest workman,
down to the poor.
O God, not of us only but of our seed,
bless our children among us,
to advance in wisdom as in stature,
and in favor with Thee and with men.
Thou who wouldest have us provide for our own,
and hatest the unnatural,
remember, Lord, my relations according
to the flesh;
grant me to speak peace concerning them,
and to seek their good.

Thou who willest us to make return
to our benefactors,
remember, Lord, for good,
all from whom I have received good;
keep them alive that they may be blessed
upon earth,
and deliver them not
into the will of their enemies.
Thou who hast noted
the man who neglects his own, as worse
than an infidel,
remember in Thy good pleasure
all those in my household.
Peace be to my house,
the Son of peace upon all in it.
Thou who wouldest that our righteousness exceed
the righteousness of sinners,
grant me, Lord, to love those who love me;
my own friend, and my father's friend,
and my friend's children,
never to forsake.
Thou who wouldest that we overcome
evil with good,
and pray for those who persecute us,
have pity on mine enemies, Lord,
as on myself;
and lead them together with me
to Thy heavenly kingdom.
Thou who grantest the prayers of Thy servants

one for another,
remember, Lord, for good,
and pity all those
who remember me in their prayers,
or whom I have promised to remember in mine.
Thou who acceptest diligence in every
good work,
remember, Lord, as if they prayed to Thee,
those who for any good reason
give not time to prayer.
Arise, and have mercy
on those who are in the last necessity,
for it is time that Thou hast mercy upon them,
yea the time is come.
Have mercy on them, O Lord,
as on me also, when in extremities.
Remember, Lord,
infants, children, the grown, the young,
the middle-aged, the old,
hungry, thirsty, naked, sick,
prisoners, foreigners, friendless, unburied,
all in extreme age and weakness,
possessed with devils, and tempted to suicide,
troubled by unclean spirits,
the hopeless, the sick in soul or body,
the weak-hearted,
all in prison and chains,
all under sentence of death;
orphans, widows, foreigners, travelers, voyagers,

women with child, women who give suck,
all in bitter servitude, or mines, or galleys,
or in loneliness.
Thou, Lord, shalt save both man and beast,
how excellent is Thy mercy, O God!
And the children of men shall put their trust
under the shadow of Thy wings.
The Lord bless us, and keep us,
and shew the light of His countenance upon us,
And be merciful unto us,
The Lord lift up His countenance upon us,
And give us peace!
I commend to Thee, O Lord,
my soul, and my body,
my mind, and my thoughts,
my prayers, and my vows,
my senses, and my limbs,
my words, and my works,
my life, and my death;
my brothers, and my sisters,
and their children;
my friends, my benefactors, my well-wishers,
those who have a claim on me;
my kindred, and my neighbors,
my country, and all Christendom.
I commend to Thee, Lord,
my impulses, and my startings,
my intentions, and my attempts,
my going out, and my coming in,
my sitting down, and my rising up.

Praise

Up with our hearts;
we lift them to the Lord.
O how very meet, and right, and fitting, and due,
in all, and for all,
at all times, places, manners,
in every season, every spot,
everywhere, always, altogether,
to remember Thee, to worship Thee,
to confess to Thee, to praise Thee,
to bless Thee, to hymn Thee,
to give thanks to Thee,
Maker, nourisher, guardian, governor,
preserver, worker, perfector of all,
Lord and Father,
King and God,
fountain of life and immortality,
treasure of everlasting goods.
Whom the heavens hymn,
and the heaven of heavens,
the Angels and all the heavenly powers,
one to other crying continually,—
and we the while, weak and unworthy,
under their feet,—
Holy, Holy, Holy,
Lord the God of Hosts;
full is the whole heaven,
and the whole earth,
of the majesty of Thy glory.

Blessed be the glory of the Lord
out of His place,
for His Godhead, His mysteriousness,
His height, His sovereignty, His almightiness,
His eternity, His providence.
The Lord is my strength, my stony rock,
and my defense,
my deliverer, my succor, my buckler,
the horn also of my salvation and my refuge.

THE SECOND DAY

Introduction

My voice shalt Thou hear betimes, O Lord,
early in the morning
will I direct my prayer unto Thee,
and will look up.
Blessed art Thou, O Lord,
who didst create the firmament of heaven,
the heavens and the heaven of heavens,
the heavenly powers,
Angels, Archangels,
Cherubim, Seraphim,
waters above the heavens,
mists and exhalations,
for showers, dew, hail, snow as wool,
hoarfrost as ashes, ice as morsels,
clouds from the ends of the earth,

lightnings, thunders, winds out of Thy treasures,
storms;
waters beneath the heavens,
for drinking and for bathing.

Confession

I will confess my sins,
and the sins of my fathers,
for I have transgressed and neglected
Thee, O Lord,
and walked perversely before Thee.
Set not, O Lord, set not my misdeeds
before Thee,
nor my life in the light of Thy countenance,
but pardon the iniquity of Thy servant,
according to Thy great mercy;
as Thou hast been merciful to him from a child,
even so now.
I have sinned, what shall I do unto Thee,
O Thou preserver of men?
Why hast Thou set me as a mark against Thee,
so that I am a burden to myself?
O pardon my transgression,
and take away mine iniquity.
Deliver me from going down to the pit,
for Thou hast found a ransom.
Have mercy on me, Son of David,
Lord, help me.

Yea, Lord, even the dogs eat of the crumbs
which fall from their masters' table.
Have patience with me, Lord,
yet I have not wherewith to pay,
I confess to Thee;
forgive me the whole debt, I beseech Thee.
How long wilt Thou forget me, O Lord?
forever?
How long wilt Thou hide Thy face from me?
How long shall I seek counsel in my soul,
and be vexed in my heart day and night?
How long shall mine enemies triumph over me?
Consider and hear me, O Lord my God,
lighten mine eyes that I sleep not in death,
lest mine enemy say I have prevailed against him,
for if I be cast down, they that trouble me will
rejoice at it;
but my trust is in Thy mercy.

Prayer for Grace

(The Ten Commandments)

Remove from me
1. all iniquity and profaneness, superstition,
and hypocrisy.
2. worship of idols, of persons.
3. rash oath, and curse.
4. neglect or indecency of worship.
5. haughtiness and recklessness.

6. strife and wrath.
7. passion and corruption.
8. indolence and fraud.
9. lying and injuriousness.
10. every evil notion, every impure thought, every base desire, every unseemly thought.

Grant to me,

1. to be religious and pious.
2. to worship and serve.
3. to bless and swear truly.
4. to confess meetly in the congregation.
5. affection and obedience.
6. patience and good temper.
7. purity and soberness.
8. contentedness and goodness.
9. truth and incorruptness.
10. good thoughts, perseverance to the end.

Profession

I believe in God,

1. the Father, Almighty, Maker of heaven and earth.
2. And in Jesus Christ, His Only-begotten Son, our Lord,
   (1) conceived of the Holy Ghost,
   (2) born of Mary, ever-virgin,
   (3) suffered under Pontius Pilate,
   (4) crucified,

    (5) dead,
    (6) buried.—
    (1) descended into hell,
    (2) risen from the dead,
    (3) ascended into heaven,
    (4) sat down on the right hand,
    (5) to return thence,
    (6) to judge both quick and dead.
3. And in the Holy Ghost,
    (1) The Holy Church,
    (2) Catholic,
    (3) communion of saints,
    (4) remission of sins,
    (5) resurrection of flesh,
    (6) life everlasting.

And now, Lord, what is my hope?
Truly my hope is even in Thee;
in Thee, O Lord, have I trusted,
    let me never be confounded.

Intercession

Let us pray God,
  for the whole creation;
  for the supply of seasons,
  healthy, fruitful, peaceful;
  for the whole race of mankind;
  for those who are not Christians;
for the conversion of Atheists, the ungodly;

Gentiles, Turks, and Jews;
for all Christians;
for restoration of all
who languish in errors and sins;
for confirmation of all
who have been granted truth and grace;
for succor and comfort of all
who are dispirited, infirm, distressed, unsettled,
men and women;
for thankfulness and sobriety in all
who are hearty, healthy, prosperous, quiet,
men and women;
for the Catholic Church,
its establishment and increase;
for the Eastern,
its deliverance and union;
for the Western,
its adjustment and peace;
for the British,
the supply of what is wanting in it,
the strengthening of what remains in it;
for the episcopate, presbytery, Christian people;
for the states of the inhabited world;
for Christian states,
far off, near at hand;
for our own;
for all in rule;
for our divinely-guarded king,
the queen and the prince;
for those who have place in the court;

for Parliament and judicature,
army and police,
commons and their leaders,
farmers, graziers, fishers, merchants,
traders, and mechanics,
down to mean workmen, and the poor,
for the rising generation;
for the good nurture of all the royal
family,
of the young ones of the nobility;
for all in universities, in inns of court,
in schools in town or country,
in apprenticeships;
for those who have a claim on me from
relationship,
for brothers and sisters,
that God's blessing may be on them,
and on their children;
or from benefits conferred,
that Thy recompence may be on all
who have benefited me,
who have ministered to me in carnal things;
or from trust placed in me,
for all whom I have educated,
all whom I have ordained:
for my college, my parish,
Southwell, St. Paul's, Westminster,
Dioceses of Chichester, Ely, and my present,
clergy, people, helps, governments,

the deanery in the chapel royal,
the almonry,
the colleges committed to me;
or from natural kindness,
for all who love me,
though I know them not;
or from Christian love;
for those who hate me without cause,
some too, even on account of truth
and righteousness;
or from neighborhood,
for all who dwell near me
peaceably and harmlessly;
or from promise,
for all whom I have promised to remember
in my prayers;
or from mutual offices,
for all who remember me in their prayers,
and ask of me the same;
or from stress of engagements,
for all who on sufficient reasons fail to call
upon Thee;
for all who have no intercessor
in their own behalf;
for all who at present are in agony
of extreme necessity or deep affliction;
for all who are attempting any good work
which will bring glory to the Name of God
or some great good to the Church;

for all who act nobly
either toward things sacred or toward the poor;
for all who have ever been offended by me
either in word or in deed.
God have mercy on me and bless me;
God shew the light of His countenance upon me
and pity me.
God bless me, even our God,
God bless me and receive my prayer;
O direct my life toward Thy commandments,
hallow my soul,
purify my body,
correct my thoughts,
cleanse my desires,
soul and body, mind and spirit,
heart and reins.
Renew me thoroughly, O God,
for, if Thou wilt, Thou canst.

Praise

The Lord, the Lord God,
merciful and pitiful,
long-suffering and full of pity, and true,
keeping pity for thousands,
taking away iniquities
and unrighteousnesses and sins;
not clearing the guilty one,
bringing sins of fathers upon children.
I will bless the Lord at all times,

His praise shall ever be in my mouth.
Glory to God in the highest,
and on earth peace,
goodwill toward men.

The Angels,	guardianship;
Archangels,	glory;
Powers,	marvels;
Thrones,	judgment;
Dominions,	beneficence;
Principalities,	government;
Authorities,	against devils;
Cherubim,	knowledge;
Seraphim,	love.

THE THIRD DAY

Introduction

O God, Thou art my God,
early will I seek Thee.
Blessed art Thou, O Lord,
who gatheredst the water into the sea,
and broughtest to sight the earth,
and madest to sprout
herb and fruit tree.
There are the depths and the sea as on an heap,
lakes, rivers, springs;
earth, continent, and isles,
mountains, hills, and valleys;

glebe, meadows, glades,
green pasture, corn, and hay;
herbs and flowers
for food, enjoyment, medicine;
fruit trees bearing
wine, oil, and spices,
and trees for wood;
and things beneath the earth,
stones, metals, minerals, coal,
blood and fire, and vapor of smoke.

Confession

Who can understand his errors?
Cleanse Thou me from secret faults.
Keep back Thy servant also from
presumptuous sins,
lest they have the dominion over me.
For Thy Name's sake,
be merciful unto my sin,
for it is great.
My iniquities have taken such hold upon me
that I am not able to look up,
yea, they are more in number than the hairs of my
head,
and my heart hath failed me.
Be pleased, O Lord, to deliver me.
Make haste, O Lord, to help me.
Magnify Thy mercies upon me,
O Thou who savest them that trust in Thee.

I said, Lord, have mercy upon me,
heal my soul, for I have sinned against Thee;
I have sinned, but I am confounded,
and I turn from my evil ways,
and I turn unto mine own heart,
and with my whole heart I turn unto Thee;
and I seek Thy face,
and I beseech Thee, saying,
I have sinned, I have committed iniquity,
I have done unjustly.
I know, O Lord, the plague of my heart,
and lo, I turn to Thee with all my heart,
and with all my strength.
And Thou, O Lord, now from Thy
dwelling-place,
and from the glorious throne of Thy kingdom
in heaven,
O hear the prayer
and the supplication of Thy servant;
and be propitious toward Thy servant
and heal his soul.
O God, be merciful to me a sinner,
be merciful to me the chief of sinners.
Father, I have sinned against heaven,
and before Thee,
and am no more worthy to be called Thy son,
make me one of Thy hired servants;
make me one, or even the last,
or the least among all.
What profit is there in my blood,

when I go down to the pit?
shall the dust give thanks unto Thee?
or shall it declare Thy truth?
Hear, O Lord, and have mercy upon me;
Lord, be Thou my helper;
turn my heaviness into joy,
my dreamings into earnestness,
my falls into clearings of myself,
my guilt, my offense into indignation,
my sin into fear,
my transgression into vehement desire,
my unrighteousness into strictness,
my pollution into revenge.

Prayer for Grace

Hosanna in the highest.
Remember me, O Lord,
with the favor that Thou bearest unto
Thy people,
O visit me with Thy salvation;
that I may see the felicity of Thy chosen,
and rejoice in the gladness of Thy people,
and give thanks with Thine inheritance.
There is glory which shall be revealed;
for when the Judge cometh,
some shall see Thy face cheerful,
and shall be placed on the right,
and shall hear those most welcome words,

"Come, ye blessed."
They shall be caught up in clouds
to meet the Lord;
they shall enter into gladness,
they shall enjoy the sight of Him,
they shall be ever with Him.
These alone, only these are blessed
among the sons of men.
O to me the meanest grant the meanest place,
there under their feet;
under the feet of Thine elect,
the meanest among them.
And that this may be,
let me find grace in Thy sight
to have grace,   (Heb. xii.28)
so as to serve Thee acceptably
with reverence and godly fear.
Let me find that second grace,
not to receive in vain   (2 Cor. vi.1)
the first grace,
not to come short of it; (Heb. xii.15)
yea, not to neglect it, (1 Tim. iv.14)
so as to fall from it,   (Gal. v.4)
but to stir it up,   (2 Tim. i.6)
so as to increase in it, (2 Pet. iii.18)
yea, to abide in it
till the end of my life.
And O, perfect for me what is lacking
of Thy gifts,

of faith,   help Thou mine unbelief,
of hope,   establish my trembling hope,
of love,   kindle its smoking flax.
        Shed abroad Thy love in my heart,
              so that I may love Thee,
      my friend in Thee, my enemy for Thee.
O Thou who givest grace to the humble-minded,
      also give me grace to be humble-minded.
O Thou who never failest those who fear Thee,
            my Fear and my Hope,
          let me fear one thing only,
      the fearing ought more than Thee.
      As I would that men should do to me
            so may I do to them;
not to have thoughts beyond what I should think,
      but to have thoughts unto sobriety.
        Shine on those who sit in darkness,
            and the shadow of death;
      guide our feet into the way of peace,
      that we may have the same thoughts
              one with another,
        rightly to divide, rightly to walk,
                  to edify,
        with one accord, with one mouth
              to glorify God;
            and if ought otherwise,
            to walk in the same rule
          as far as we have attained;
              to maintain order,
          decency and stedfastness.

Profession

Godhead, paternal love, power,
providence:
salvation, anointing, adoption,
lordship;
conception, birth, passion,
cross, death, burial,
descent, resurrection, ascent,
sitting, return, judgment;
Breath and Holiness,
calling from the Universal,
hallowing in the Universal,
communion of saints, and of saintly things,
resurrection,
life eternal.

Intercession

Hosanna on the earth.
Remember, O Lord,
to crown the year with Thy goodness;
for the eyes of all look toward Thee,
and Thou givest their food in due season.
Thou openest Thine hand,
and fillest all things living with plenteousness.
And on us, O Lord, vouchsafe
the blessings of heaven and the dew above,
blessings of fountains and the deep beneath,
courses of sun, conjunctions of moons,

summits of eastern mountains,
of the everlasting hills,
fullness of the earth and of produce thereof,
good seasons, wholesome weather,
full crops, plenteous fruits,
health of body, peaceful times,
mild government, kind laws,
wise councils, equal judgments,
loyal obedience, vigorous justice,
fertility in resources, fruitfulness in begetting,
ease in bearing, happiness in offspring,
careful nurture, sound training,
that our sons may grow up as the young plants,
our daughters as the polished corners
of the temple,
that our garners may be full and plenteous
with all manner of store,
that our sheep may bring forth thousands
and ten thousands in our streets:
that there be no decay,
no leading into captivity
and no complaining in our streets.

Praise

Thou, O Lord, art praised in Zion,
and unto Thee shall the vow be performed
in Jerusalem.
Thou art worthy, O Lord our God,

the Holy One,
to receive glory, and honor, and power.
Thou that hearest the prayer,
unto Thee shall all flesh come,
my flesh shall come.
My misdeeds prevail against me,
O be Thou merciful unto our sins;
that I may come and give thanks
with all Thy works,
and bless Thee with Thy holy ones.
O Lord, open Thou my lips,
and my mouth shall shew forth Thy praise.
My soul doth praise the Lord,
for the goodness He hath done
to the whole creation,
and to the whole race of men;
for Thy mercies toward myself,
soul, body, and estate,
gifts of grace, nature, and fortune;
for all benefits received,
for all successes, now or heretofore,
for any good thing done;
for health, credit, competency,
safety, gentle estate, quiet.
Thou hast not cut off as a weaver my life,
nor from day even to night made an end of me.
He hath vouchsafed me life and breath
until this hour,
from childhood, youth, and hitherto

even unto age.
He holdeth our soul in life
and suffereth not our feet to slip;
rescuing me from perils, sicknesses,
poverty, bondage,
public shame, evil chances;
keeping me from perishing in my sins,
fully waiting my conversion,
leaving in me return into my heart,
remembrance of my latter end,
shame, horror, grief,
for my past sins;
fuller and larger, larger and fuller,
more and still more, O my Lord,
storing me with good hope
of their remission,
through repentance and its works,
in the power of the thrice-holy Keys,
and the mysteries in Thy Church.
Wherefore day by day
for these Thy benefits toward me,
which I remember,—
wherefore also for others very many
which I have let slip
from their number, from my forgetfulness,—
for those which I wished, knew and asked,
and those I asked not, knew not, wished not,—
I confess and give thanks to Thee,
I bless and praise Thee, as is fit, and every day.

And I pray with my whole soul,
and with my whole mind I pray.
Glory be to Thee, O Lord, glory to
Thee;
glory to Thee,
and glory to Thine All-holy Name,
for all Thy Divine perfections in them;
for Thine incomprehensible and
unimaginable goodness,
and Thy pity toward sinners
and unworthy men,
and toward me of all sinners
far the most unworthy.
Yea, O Lord,
for this, and for the rest,
Glory to Thee,
and praise, and blessing, and thanksgiving,
with the voices and concert of voices
of Angels and of men,
of all Thy saints in heaven,
and all Thy creatures in heaven or earth,
and of me, beneath their feet,
unworthy and wretched sinner,
Thy abject creature,
now, in this day and hour,
and every day till my last breath,
and till the end of the world,
and for ages upon ages.

THE FOURTH DAY

Introduction

I have thought upon Thee, O Lord,
when I was waking,
for Thou hast been my helper.
Blessed art Thou, O Lord,
who madest the two Lights, Sun and Moon,
greater and lesser,
and the stars
for light, for signs, for seasons,
spring, summer, autumn, winter,
days, weeks, months, years,
to rule over day and night.

Confession

Behold, Thou art angry, for we have sinned.
We are all as an unclean thing,
and all our righteousnesses
as filthy rags.
We all do fade as a leaf,
and our iniquities, like the wind,
have taken us away.
But now, O Lord, Thou art our Father;
we are clay, all Thy handiwork.
Be not wroth very sore,
nor remember iniquity forever;

behold, see, we beseech Thee,
we are all Thy people.
O Lord, though our iniquities testify against us,
do Thou it for Thy Name's sake:
for our backslidings are many;
we have sinned against Thee.
Yet Thou, O Lord, art in the midst of us,
and we are called by Thy Name;
leave us not.
O Hope of Israel,
The Saviour thereof in time of trouble,
why shouldest Thou be as a stranger in
the land,
and as a wayfaring man that turneth aside
to tarry for a night?
why shouldest Thou be as a man astonished,
as a mighty man that cannot save?
Be merciful to our unrighteousnesses,
and our iniquities remember no more.
Lord, I am carnal,
sold under sin;
there dwelleth in me, that is, in my flesh,
no good thing;
for the good that I would, I do not,
but the evil which I would not, that I do.
I consent unto the law that it is good,
I delight in it after the inner man;
but I see another law in my members,
warring against the law of my mind,
and enslaving me to the law of sin.

Wretched man that I am,
who shall deliver me from the body of this death?
I thank God through Jesus Christ,
that where sin abounded,
grace hath much more abounded.
O Lord, Thy goodness leadeth me to repentance:
O give me sometime repentance
to recover me from the snare of the devil,
who am taken captive by him
at his will.
Sufficient for me the past time of my life
to have done the will of lusts,
walking in lasciviousness, reveling, drunkenness,
and in other excess of profligacy.
O Lamb without blemish and without spot,
who hast redeemed me with Thy precious Blood,
in that very Blood pity me and save me;
in that Blood,
and in that very Name,
besides which is none other under heaven
given among men,
by which we must be saved.
O God, Thou knowest my foolishness,
and my sins are not hid from Thee.
Lord, Thou knowest all my desire,
and my groaning is not hid from Thee.
Let not them that trust in Thee,
O Lord God of hosts,
be ashamed for my cause;
let not those that seek Thee be confounded

through me,
O Lord God of Israel.
Take me out of the mire that I sink not;
O let me be delivered from them that hate me
and out of the deep waters.
Let not the water flood drown me,
neither let the deep swallow me up,
and let not the pit shut her mouth upon me.

Prayer for Grace

[Defend me from]
(against seven deadly sins)

pride	Amorite;
envy	Hittite;
wrath	Perizzite;
gluttony	Girgashite;
lechery	Hivite;

(covetousness)

the cares of life	Canaanite;

(sloth)

lukewarm indifference	Jebusite.

[Give me]
humility, pitifulness, patience,
sobriety, purity, contentment, ready zeal.
One thing have I desired of the Lord
which I will require,
that I may dwell in the house of the Lord
all the days of my life,
to behold the fair beauty of the Lord,

and to visit His temple.
Two things have I required of Thee, O Lord,
deny Thou me not before I die;
remove far from me vanity and lies;
give me neither poverty nor riches,
feed me with food convenient for me;
lest I be full and deny Thee
and say, Who is the Lord?
or lest I be poor and steal,
and take the Name of my God in vain.
Let me learn to abound,
let me learn to suffer need,
in whatsoever state I am,
therewith to be content.
For nothing earthly, temporal, mortal,
to long nor to wait.
Grant me a happy life
in piety, gravity, purity,
in all things good and fair,
in cheerfulness, in health, in credit,
in competency, in safety, in gentle estate, in quiet;
a happy death,
a deathless happiness.

Profession

I believe
in the Father, benevolent affection;
in the Almighty, saving power;

in the Creator, providence
for guarding, ruling, perfecting the universe.
In Jesus, salvation,
in Christ, anointing;
in the Only-begotten Son, sonship,
in the Lord, a master's treatment,
in His conception and birth,
the cleansing of our unclean conception and birth;
in His sufferings, which we owed,
that we might not pay;
in His cross the curse of the law removed;
in His death the sting of death;
in His burial eternal destruction in the tomb;
in His descent, whither we ought,
that we might not go;
in His resurrection,
as the first fruits of them that sleep;
in His ascent, to prepare a place for us;
in His sitting, to appear and intercede;
in His return, to take unto Him His own;
in His judgment, to render to each
according to his works.
In the Holy Ghost, power from on high,
transforming unto sanctity
from without and invisibly,
yet inwardly and evidently.
In the Church, a body mystical
of those called out of the whole world,
unto intercourse in faith and holiness.

In the communion of saints,
members of this body,
a mutual participation in holy things,
for confidence of remission of sins,
for hope of resurrection, of translation,
to life everlasting.

Intercession

And I have hoped in Thy mercy
from everlasting to everlasting.
How excellent is Thy mercy, O Lord.
If I have hope, it is in Thy mercy;
O let me not be disappointed of my hope.
Moreover we beseech Thee,
remember all, Lord, for good;
have pity upon all, O Sovereign Lord,
be reconciled with us all.
Give peace to the multitudes of Thy people;
scatter offenses;
abolish wars;
stop the uprisings of heresies.
Thy peace and love
vouchsafe to us, O God our Saviour,
the Hope of all the ends of the
earth.
Remember to crown the year
with Thy goodness;
for the eyes of all wait upon Thee,
and Thou givest them their meat in due season.

Thou openest Thy hand,
and fillest all things living with plenteousness.
Remember Thy Holy Church,
from one end of the earth to the other;
and give her peace,
whom Thou hast redeemed with Thy
precious Blood;
and establish her
unto the end of the world.
Remember those who bear fruit, and act nobly,
in Thy Holy Churches,
and who remember the poor and needy;
recompense to them
Thy rich and heavenly gifts;
vouchsafe to them,
for things earthly, heavenly,
for corruptible, incorruptible,
for temporal, eternal.
Remember those who are in virginity,
and purity and ascetic life;
also those who live in honorable marriage,
in Thy reverence and fear.
Remember every Christian soul
in affliction, distress, and trial,
and in need of Thy pity and succor;
also our brethren in captivity, prison, chains,
and bitter bondage;
supplying return to the wandering,
health to the sick,
deliverance to the captives.

Remember religious and faithful kings,
whom Thou hast given to rule
upon the earth;
and especially remember, Lord,
our divinely-guarded king;
strengthen his kingdom,
subdue to him all adversaries,
speak good things to his heart,
for Thy Church, and all Thy people.
Vouchsafe to him deep and undisturbed peace,
that in his serenity
we may lead a quiet and peaceable life
with all godliness and honesty.
Remember, Lord, all power
and authority,
our brethren in the court,
those who are chief in council and judgment,
and all by land and sea
waging Thy wars for us.
Moreover, Lord, remember graciously
our holy Fathers,
the honorable presbytery, and all the clergy,
rightly dividing the word of truth,
and rightly walking in it.
Remember, Lord, our brethren around us,
and praying with us in this holy hour,
for their zeal and earnestness' sake.
Remember also those who on fair reasons
are away,
and pity them and us

in the multitude of Thy pity.
Fill our garners with all manner of store,
preserve our marriages in peace and concord,
nourish our infants,
lead forward our youth,
sustain our aged,
comfort the weak-hearted,
gather together the scattered,
restore the wanderers,
and knit them to Thy Holy Catholic Apostolic
Church.
Set free the troubled
with unclean spirits,
voyage with the voyagers,
travel with the travelers,
stand forth for the widow,
shield the orphan,
rescue the captive,
heal the sick.
Those who are on trial, in mines, in exile,
in galleys,
in whatever affliction, necessity, and emergence,
remember, O God;
and all who need Thy great mercy;
and those who love us,
and those who hate;
and those who have desired us unworthy
to make mention of them in our prayers;
and all Thy people remember, O Lord, our God,
and upon all pour out Thy rich pity,

to all performing their requests for salvation;
and those of whom we have not made mention,
through ignorance, forgetfulness, or number
of names,
do Thou Thyself remember, O God,
who knowest the stature and appellation of each,
who knowest every one from his mother's womb.
For Thou art, O Lord, the Succor of the
succorless,
the Hope of the hopeless,
The Saviour of the tempest-tossed,
the Harbor of the voyager,
the Physician of the sick,
do Thou Thyself become all things to all men.
O Thou who knowest each man and his petition,
each house, and its need,
deliver, O Lord, this city,
and all the country in which we sojourn,
from plague, famine, earthquake, flood,
fire, sword, hostile invasion,
and civil war.
End the schisms of the Churches,
quench the haughty cries of the nations,
and receive us all into Thy kingdom,
acknowledging us as sons of light;
and Thy peace and love
vouchsafe to us, O Lord, our God.
Remember O Lord, our God,
all spirits and all flesh

which we have remembered, and which
we have not.
And the close of our life,
Lord, Lord, direct in peace,
Christianly, acceptably, and, should it please Thee,
painlessly,
gathering us together under the feet
of Thine elect,
when Thou wilt and how Thou wilt,
only without shame and sins.
The brightness of the Lord our God be upon us,
prosper Thou the work of our hands upon us,
O prosper Thou our handiwork.
Be, Lord,
within me to strengthen me,
without me to guard me,
over me to shelter me,
beneath me to establish me,
before me to guide me,
after me to forward me,
round about me to secure me.

Praise

Blessed art Thou, Lord God of Israel,
our Father,
from everlasting to everlasting.
Thine, O Lord,
is the greatness and the power,

the triumph and the victory,
the praise and the strength,
for Thou rulest over all
in heaven and on earth.
At Thy face every king is troubled,
and every nation.
Thine, O Lord, is the kingdom
and the supremacy over all,
and over all rule.
With Thee is wealth, and glory is from
Thy countenance;
Thou rulest over all, O Lord,
the Ruler of all rule;
and in Thine hand is strength and power,
and in Thine hand to give to all things
greatness and strength.
And now, Lord, we confess to Thee
and we praise Thy glorious Name.

THE FIFTH DAY

Introduction

We are satisfied with Thy mercy, O Lord,
in the morning.
Blessed art Thou, O Lord
who broughtest forth from the water
creeping things of life,
and whales,
and winged fowl.

Be Thou exalted, O God, above the heavens,
    and Thy glory above all the earth.
    By Thy Ascension, O Lord,
        draw us too after Thee,
    that we savor of what is above,
        not of things on the earth.

By the marvelous mystery
of the Holy Body and precious Blood,
    on the evening of this day,
        Lord, have mercy.

Confession

Thou who hast said,
    "As I live, saith the Lord,
    I will not the death of a sinner,
but that the ungodly return from his way
        and live;
    turn ye, turn ye from your wicked way,
    for why will ye die, O house of Israel?"
        turn us, O Lord, to Thee,
        and so shall we be turned.
    Turn us from all our ungodlinesses,
and let them not be to us for punishments.
I have sinned, I have committed iniquity,
        I have done wickedly,
from Thy precepts, and Thy judgments.
    To Thee, O Lord, righteousness,
        and to me confusion of face,
            as at this day,

in our despicableness,
wherewith Thou hast despised us.
Lord, to us confusion of face,
and to our rulers
who have sinned against Thee.
Lord, in all things is Thy righteousness,
unto all Thy righteousness;
let then Thine anger and Thy fury be
turned away,
and cause Thy face to shine
upon Thy servant.
O my God, incline Thine ear and hear,
open Thine eyes and see my desolation.
O Lord, hear, O Lord forgive,
O Lord hearken and do;
defer not for Thine own sake, O my God,
for Thy servant is called by Thy Name.
In many things we offend all;
Lord, let Thy mercy rejoice against Thy
judgment in my sins.
If I say I have no sin, I deceive myself,
and the truth is not in me;
but I confess my sins many and grievous,
and Thou, O Lord, art faithful and just,
to forgive me my sins when I confess them.
Yea, for this too
I have an Advocate with Thee to Thee,
Thy Only-begotten Son, the Righteous.
May He be the propitiation for my sins,
who is also for the whole world.

Will the Lord cast off forever?
and will He be no more entreated?
Is His mercy clean gone forever?
and is His promise come utterly to an end
forevermore?
Hath God forgotten to be gracious?
and will He shut up His loving-kindness
in displeasure?
And I said, It is mine own infirmity;
but I will remember the years of the right hand
of the Most High.

Prayer for Grace

[Give me grace]
to put aside every weight,
and the sin that doth so easily beset us;
all filthiness
and superfluity of naughtiness,
lust of the flesh, of the eyes,
pride of life,
every motion of flesh and spirit
alienated from the will of Thy sanctity:
to be poor in spirit,
that I have a portion in the kingdom of heaven;
to mourn, that I be comforted;
to be meek, that I inherit the earth;
to hunger and thirst for righteousness,
that I be filled;
to be pitiful, that I be pitied;

to be pure in heart, that I see God;
to be a peace-maker that I be called the
son of God;
to be prepared for persecutions and revilings
for righteousness' sake,
that my reward be in heaven,—
all this, grant to me, O Lord.

Profession

I, coming to God,
believe that He is,
and that He is a rewarder of them
that diligently seek Him.
I know that my Redeemer liveth,
that He is Christ, the Son of the Living God,
that He is truly the Saviour of the world,
that He came into the world to save sinners,
of whom I am chief.
Through the grace of Jesus Christ
we believe that we shall be saved
even as our fathers.
I know that my skin shall rise up upon the earth,
which undergoeth these things.
I believe to see the goodness of the Lord
in the land of the living.
Our heart shall rejoice in Him,
because we have hoped in His Holy Name,
in the Name of the Father,

of the Saviour, Mediator, Intercessor, Redeemer,
of the two-fold Comforter,
under the figures of the Lamb and the Dove.
Let Thy merciful kindness, O Lord, be upon us,
according as we do put our trust in Thee.

Intercession

Let us beseech the Lord in peace,
for the heavenly peace,
and the salvation of our souls;—
for the peace of the whole world;
for the stability of God's Holy Churches,
and the union of them all;—
for this holy house,
and those who enter it with faith and
reverence;
for our holy Fathers,
the honorable presbytery,
the diaconate in Christ,
and all, both clergy and people;—
for this holy retreat, and all the city and country,
and all the faithful who dwell therein;—
for salubrious weather, fruitfulness of earth,
and peaceful times;—
for voyagers, travelers,
those who are in sickness, toil, and captivity,
and for their salvation.
Aid, save, pity, and preserve them,
O God, in Thy grace.

Making mention
of the All-holy, undefiled, and more than blessed
Mary, Mother of God, and Ever-Virgin,
with all saints,
let us commend ourselves, and each other,
and all our life,
to Christ our God.
To Thee, O Lord, for it is fitting,
be glory, honor, and worship.
The grace of our Lord, Jesus Christ,
and the love of God,
and the communion of the Holy Ghost,
be with me, and with all of us. Amen.
I commend me and mine,
and all that belongs to me,
to Him who is able to keep me without falling,
and to place me immaculate
before the presence of His glory,
to the only wise God and our Saviour;
to whom be glory and greatness,
strength and authority,
both now and for all ages. Amen.

Praise

O Lord, my Lord,
for my being, life, reason,
for nurture, protection, guidance,
for education, civil rights, religion,
for Thy gifts of grace, nature, fortune,

for redemption, regeneration, catechising,
for my call, recall, yea, many calls besides;
for Thy forbearance, long-suffering,
long long-suffering
toward me,
many seasons, many years, up to this time;
for all good things received, successes granted me,
good things done;
for the use of things present,
for Thy promise, and my hope
of the enjoyment of good things to come;
for my parents honest and good,
teachers kind,
benefactors never to be forgotten,
religious intimates congenial,
hearers thoughtful,
friends sincere,
domestics faithful,
for all who have advantaged me,
by writings, homilies, converse,
prayers, patterns, rebukes, injuries;
for all these, and all others
which I know, which I know not,
open, hidden,
remembered, forgotten,
done when I wished, when I wished not,
I confess to Thee and will confess,
I bless Thee and will bless,
I give thanks to Thee and will give thanks,
all the days of my life.

Who am I, or what is my father's house,
that Thou shouldest look upon a dead dog,
the like of me?
What reward shall I give unto the Lord
for all the benefits which He hath done unto me?
What thanks can I recompense unto God,
for all He hath spared and borne with me
until now?
Holy, Holy, Holy,
worthy art Thou,
O Lord and our God, the Holy One,
to receive the glory, and the honor,
and the power,
for Thou hast made all things,
and for Thy pleasure they are,
and were created.

THE SIXTH DAY

Introduction

Early shall my prayer come before Thee.
Blessed art Thou, O Lord,
who broughtest forth of the earth,
wild beasts, cattle,
and all the reptiles,
for food, clothing, help;
and madest man after Thine image,
to rule the earth,
and blessedst him.

The fore-counsel, fashioning hand,
breath of life, image of God,
appointment over the works,
charge to the Angels concerning him,
paradise.—
Heart, reins, eyes, ears, tongue, hands, feet,
life, sense, reason, spirit, free will,
memory, conscience,
the revelation of God, writing of the law,
oracles of prophets, music of psalms,
instruction of proverbs, experience of histories,
worship of sacrifices.

Blessed art Thou, O Lord,
for Thy great and precious promise
on this day,
concerning the Life-giving Seed,
and for its fulfilment in fullness of the times
on this day.

Blessed art Thou, O Lord,
for the holy Passion
of this day.
O by Thy salutary sufferings
on this day,
save us, O Lord.

Confession

I have withstood Thee, Lord,
but I return to Thee;
for I have fallen by mine iniquity.

But I take with me words,
and I return unto Thee and say,
Take away all iniquity and receive us graciously,
so will we render the calves of our lips.
Spare us, Lord, spare,
and give not Thine heritage to reproach,
to Thine enemies.

Lord, Lord, be propitious;
cease, I beseech Thee;
by whom shall Jacob arise?
for he is small.
Repent, O Lord, for this,
and this shall not be.

While observing lying vanities
I forsook my own mercy,
and am cast out of Thy sight.
When my soul fainted within me,
I remembered the Lord;
yet will I look again toward Thy Holy Temple,
Thou hast brought up my life from corruption.

Who is a God like unto Thee,
that pardoneth iniquity
to the remnant of His heritage?
He retaineth not His anger forever,
because He delighteth in mercy.
Turn again and have compassion
upon us, O Lord,
subdue our iniquities,

and cast all our sins into the depths of the sea,
according to Thy truth,
and according to Thy mercy.

O Lord, I have heard Thy speech and was afraid,
in wrath remember mercy.
Behold me, Lord, clothed in filthy garments;
behold Satan standing at my right hand;
yet, O Lord, by the Blood of Thy covenant,
by the fountain opened for sin and for
uncleanness,
take away my iniquity,
and cleanse me from my sin.

Save me as a brand
plucked out of the fire.
Father, forgive me, for I knew not,
truly I knew not, what I did
in sinning against Thee.
Lord, remember me
when Thou comest in Thy kingdom.
Lord, lay not mine enemies' sins to their charge;
Lord, lay not my own to mine.
By Thy sweat bloody and clotted,
Thy soul in agony,
Thy head crowned with thorns,
bruised with staves,
Thine eyes swimming with tears,
Thine ears full of insults,
Thy mouth moistened with vinegar and gall,
Thy face dishonorably stained with spitting,

Thy neck weighed down with the burden
of the cross,
Thy back ploughed with the wheals and gashes
of the scourge,
The hands and feet stabbed through,
Thy strong cry, "Eli, Eli,"
Thy heart pierced with the spear,
the water and blood thence flowing,
Thy Body broken,
Thy Blood poured out,
Lord, forgive the offense of Thy servant,
and cover all his sins.
Turn away all Thy displeasure,
and turn Thyself from Thy wrathful
indignation.
Turn me then, O God our Saviour,
and let Thine anger cease from us.
Wilt Thou be displeased at us forever,
and stretch out Thy wrath from one generation
to another?
Wilt Thou not turn again and quicken us,
that Thy people may rejoice in Thee?
Shew us Thy mercy, O Lord,
and grant us Thy salvation.

Prayer for Grace

. . . . .

the works of the flesh,
adultery, fornication, uncleanness, lasciviousness,

idolatry, witchcraft,
enmities, strifes,
emulations, heats,
quarrels, parties,
heresies, envyings, murders,
drunkennesses, revelings, and such like.

. . . . . .

the fruits of the Spirit,
love, joy, peace,
long-suffering, gentleness, goodness,
faith, meekness, temperance;
the spirit of wisdom, of understanding,
of counsel, of might,
of knowledge, of godliness,
of fear of the Lord:—
and the gifts of the Spirit,
the word of wisdom, of knowledge,
faith, gifts of healing, working of miracles,
prophecy, discerning of spirits,
kinds of tongues, interpretation of tongues.
May Thy strong hand, O Lord,
be ever my defense;
Thy mercy in Christ
my salvation;
Thy all-veritable word,
my instructor;
the grace of Thy Life-bringing Spirit,
my consolation
all along, and at last.

The Soul of Christ hallow me,
and the Body strengthen me,
and the Blood ransom me,
and the Water wash me,
and the Bruises heal me,
and the Sweat refresh me,
and the Wound hide me.
The peace of God
which passeth all understanding,
keep my heart and thoughts
in the knowledge and the love of God.

Profession

I believe
that Thou hast created me;
despise not the work of Thine own hands;—
that Thou madest me after Thine image
and likeness,
suffer not Thy likeness to be blotted out;—
that Thou hast redeemed me in Thy Blood,
suffer not the cost of that redemption to perish;
that Thou hast called me Christian
after Thy Name,
disdain not Thine own title;
that Thou hast hallowed me in regeneration,
destroy not Thy holy work;—
that Thou hast grafted me into the
good olive tree,
the member of a mystical body,

the member of Thy mystical Body,
cut not off.
O think upon Thy servant as concerning
Thy word,
wherein Thou has caused me to put my trust.
My soul hath longed for Thy salvation,
and I have good hope because of Thy word.

Intercession

[I pray]
for the prosperous advance and good condition
of all the Christian army,
against the enemies of our most holy faith;
for our holy Fathers,
and all our brotherhood in Christ;
for those who hate and those who love us,
for those who pity and those who minister to us;
for those whom we have promised
to remember in prayer;
for the liberation of captives;
for our fathers and brethren absent;
for those who voyage by sea;
for those who lie in sickness.
Let us pray also for fruitfulness of the earth;
and for every soul of orthodox Christians.
Let us bless pious kings,
orthodox high priests,
the founders of this holy retreat,
our parents,

and all our forefathers
and our brethren departed.

Praise

Thou who, on man's transgressing Thy command,
and falling,
didst not pass him by, nor leave him,
God of goodness;
but didst visit in ways manifold,
as a tender Father,
supplying him with Thy great and
precious promise,
concerning the Life-giving Seed,
opening to him the door of faith,
and of repentance unto life,
and in fullness of the times,
sending Thy Christ Himself
to take on Him the seed of Abraham;
and, in the oblation of His life,
to fulfil the law's obedience;
and, in the sacrifice of His death,
to take off the law's curse;
and, in His death,
to redeem the world;
and, in His resurrection,
to quicken it:—
O Thou, who doest all things,
whereby to bring again our race to Thee,

that it may be partaker
of Thy Divine nature and eternal glory;
who hast borne witness
to the truth of Thy gospel
by many and various wonders,
in the ever-memorable converse of Thy saints,
in their supernatural endurance of torments,
in the overwhelming conversion of all lands
to the obedience of faith,
without might, or persuasion, or compulsion:—
blessed be Thy Name,
and praised and celebrated,
and magnified, and high exalted,
and glorified, and hallowed;
its record, and its memory,
and every memorial of it,
both now and forevermore.
Worthy art Thou to take the book,
and to open the seals thereof,
for Thou wast slain, and hast redeemed us to God
by Thy Blood,
out of every kindred and tongue,
and people, and nation.
Worthy is the Lamb that was slain
to receive the power, and riches, and wisdom,
and strength, and honor, and glory, and blessing.
To Him that sitteth upon the Throne,
and to the Lamb,
be the blessing, and the honor, and the glory,

and the might,
forever and ever. Amen.
Salvation to our God, which sitteth
upon the throne,
and to the Lamb.
Amen: the blessing and the glory and the wisdom,
and the thanksgiving and the honor,
and the power and the strength,
be unto our God,
forever and ever,
Amen.

THE SEVENTH DAY

Introduction

O Lord, be gracious unto us,
we have waited for Thee;
be Thou our arm every morning,
our salvation also in the time of trouble.
Blessed art Thou, O Lord,
who restedst on the seventh day
from all Thy works,
and blessedst and sanctifiedst it:
(concerning the Sabbath,
concerning the Christian rest instead of it,
concerning the burial of Christ,
and the resting from sin,
concerning those who are already gone to rest.)

Confession

I am ashamed, and blush, O my God,
to lift up my face to Thee,
for mine iniquities are increased
over my head,
and my trespass is grown up unto the heavens;
since the days of youth
have I been in a great trespass
unto this day;
I cannot stand before Thee because of this.
My sins are more in number than the
sand of the sea,
my iniquities are multiplied,
and I not worthy to look up
and see the height of heaven,
from the number of my unrighteousnesses;
and I have no relief,
because I have provoked Thine anger,
and done evil in Thy sight;
not doing Thy will,
not keeping Thy commandments.
And now my heart kneels to Thee,
beseeching Thy goodness.
I have sinned, O Lord, I have sinned,
and I know mine iniquities;
and I ask and beseech,
remit to me, O Lord, remit to me,
and destroy me not in mine iniquities;

nor be Thou angry forever,
nor reserve evil for me;
nor condemn me
in the lowest parts of the earth.
Because Thou art God, the God of penitents,
and Thou shalt shew in me all Thy
loving-kindness;
for Thou shalt save me unworthy,
according to Thy much pity,
and I will praise Thee alway.
Lord, if Thou wilt, Thou canst cleanse me;
Lord, only say the word, and I shall be healed.
Lord, save me;
carest Thou not that we perish?
Say to me, Be of good cheer, thy sins are remitted
to thee.
Jesu, Master, have mercy on me;
Thou Son of David, Jesu, have mercy on me;
Jesu, Son of David, Son of David.
Lord, say to me, Ephphatha.
Lord, I have no man;   [John v.7]
Lord, say to me, Be loosed from thine infirmity.
Say unto my soul, I am thy salvation.
Say unto me, My grace is sufficient for thee.
Lord, how long wilt Thou be angry?
shall Thy jealousy burn like fire forever?
O, remember not our old sins;
but have mercy on us and that soon,
for we are come to great misery;
Help us, O God of our salvation;

for the glory of Thy Name.
O deliver us and be merciful unto our sins,
for Thy Name's sake.

Prayer for Grace

[O Lord, remit]
all my failings, shortcomings, falls,
offenses, trespasses, scandals,
transgressions, debts, sins,
faults, ignorances, iniquities,
impieties, unrighteousnesses, pollutions.
The guilt of them,

be gracious unto,	pardon;
remit,	forgive;
be propitious unto,	spare;
impute not,	charge not, remember not.

The stain,

pass by,	pass over;
disregard,	overlook;
hide,	wash away;
blot out,	cleanse.

The hurt,

remit,	heal,	remedy;
take off,	remove,	away with;
abolish,	annul,	disperse, annihilate;

that they be not found, that they exist not.
Supply

to faith,	virtue;
to virtue,	knowledge;

to knowledge,	continence;
to continence,	patience;
to patience,	godliness;
to godliness,	brotherly love;
to brotherly love,	charity.

That I forget not my cleansing from my
former sins,
but give diligence to make my calling
and election sure
through good works.

Profession

I believe in Thee, the Father;
behold then, if Thou art a Father and we sons,
as a father pitieth sons,
be Thou of tender mercy toward us, O Lord.
I believe in Thee, the Lord;
behold then, if Thou art Lord and we servants,
our eyes are upon Thee, our Lord,
until Thou have mercy upon us.
I believe that though we be neither sons
nor servants,
but dogs only,
yet we have leave to eat of the crumbs
that fall from Thy table.
I believe that Christ is the Lamb of God;
O Lamb of God that takest away the sins
of the world,
take Thou away mine.

I believe that Jesus Christ came into the world
to save sinners;
Thou who camest to save sinners
save Thou me, of sinners
chief and greatest.
I believe that Christ came to save what was lost;
Thou who camest to save the lost,
never suffer, O Lord, that to be lost which
Thou hast saved.
I believe that the Spirit is the Lord and
Giver of life;
Thou who gavest me a living soul,
give me that I receive not my soul in vain.
I believe that the Spirit gives grace
in His sacred things;
give me that I receive not His grace in vain,
nor hope of His sacred things.
I believe that the Spirit intercedes for us
with plaints unutterable;
grant me of His intercession and those plaints
to partake, O Lord.
Our fathers hoped in Thee,
they trusted in Thee, and Thou didst
deliver them.
They called upon Thee and were holpen,
they put their trust in Thee, and were not
confounded.
As Thou didst our fathers
in the generations of old,
so also deliver us, O Lord,
who trust in Thee.

Intercession

O Heavenly King,
confirm our faithful kings,
stablish the faith,
soften the nations,
pacify the world,
guard well this holy retreat,
and receive us in orthodox faith and repentance,
as a kind and loving Lord.
The power of the Father guide me,
the wisdom of the Son enlighten me,
the working of the Spirit quicken me.
Guard Thou my soul,
stablish my body,
elevate my senses,
direct my converse,
form my habits,
bless my actions,
fulfil my prayers,
inspire holy thoughts,
pardon the past,
correct the present,
prevent the future.

Praise

Now unto Him that is able to do
exceeding abundantly

above all that we ask or think,
according to the power that worketh in us,
to Him be glory
in the Church in Christ
unto all generations
world without end. Amen.
Blessed, and praised, and celebrated,
and magnified, and exalted, and glorified,
and hallowed,
be Thy Name, O Lord,
its record, and its memory,
and every memorial of it;
for the all-honorable senate of the Patriarchs,
the ever-venerable band of the Prophets,
the all-glorious college of the Apostles,
the Evangelists,
the all-illustrious army of the Martyrs,
the Confessors,
the assembly of Doctors,
the Ascetics,
the beauty of Virgins,
for Infants the delight of the world,—

for their faith,	their hope,
their labors,	their truth,
their blood,	their zeal,
their diligence,	their tears,
their purity,	their beauty,

Glory to Thee, O Lord, glory to Thee,
glory to Thee who didst glorify them,
among whom we too glorify Thee.

Great and marvelous are Thy works,
Lord, the God Almighty;
just and true are Thy ways,
O King of Saints.
Who shall not fear Thee, O Lord,
and glorify Thy Name?
for Thou only art holy,
for all the nations shall come and worship
before Thee,
for Thy judgments are made manifest.
Praise our God, all ye His servants,
and ye that fear Him,
both small and great,
Alleluia,
for the Lord God Omnipotent reigneth;
let us be glad and rejoice, and give honor to Him.
Behold the tabernacle of God is with men,
and He will dwell with them;
and they shall be His people,
and God Himself shall be with them,
and shall wipe away all tears from their eyes.
And there shall be no more death;
neither crying, neither pain any more,
for the former things are passed away.

Morning Prayers

ORDER OF MATIN PRAYER

Litany

Glory be to Thee, O Lord, glory to Thee.
Glory to Thee who givest me sleep
to recruit my weakness,
and to remit the toils
of this fretful flesh.
To this day and all days,
a perfect, holy, peaceful, healthy, sinless course,
Vouchsafe O Lord.

The Angel of peace, a faithful guide,
guardian of souls and bodies,
to encamp around me,
and ever to prompt what is salutary,
Vouchsafe O Lord.

Pardon and remission
of all sins and of all offenses,
Vouchsafe O Lord.

To our souls what is good and convenient,
and peace to the world,
Vouchsafe O Lord.

Repentance and strictness
for the residue of our life,
and health and peace to the end,
                    Vouchsafe O Lord.

Whatever is true, whatever is honest,
whatever just, whatever pure,
whatever lovely, whatever of good report,
if there be any virtue, if any praise,
such thoughts, such deeds,
                    Vouchsafe O Lord.

A Christian close,
without sin, without shame,
and, should it please Thee, without pain,
and a good answer
at the dreadful and fearful judgment seat
of Jesus Christ our Lord,
                    Vouchsafe O Lord.

Confession

Essence beyond essence, Nature increate,
Framer of the world,
I set Thee, Lord, before my face,
and I lift up my soul unto Thee.
I worship Thee on my knees,
and humble myself under Thy mighty hand.
I stretch forth my hands unto Thee,
my soul gaspeth unto Thee as a thirsty land.
I smite on my breast
and say with the Publican,

God be merciful to me a sinner,
the chief of sinners;
to the sinner above the Publican,
be merciful as to the Publican.
Father of mercies,
I beseech Thy fatherly affection;
despise me not,
an unclean worm, a dead dog, a putrid corpse,
despise not Thou the work of Thine own hands,
despise not Thine own image
though branded by sin.
Lord, if Thou wilt, Thou canst make me clean;
Lord, only say the word, and I shall be cleansed.
And Thou, my Saviour Christ,
Christ my Saviour,
Saviour of sinners, of whom I am chief,
despise me not, despise me not, O Lord,
despise not the cost of Thy Blood,
who am called by Thy Name;
but look on me with those eyes
with which Thou didst look upon
Magdalene at the feast,
Peter in the hall,
the thief on the wood;—
that with the thief I may entreat Thee humbly,
Remember me, Lord, in Thy kingdom;
that with Peter I may bitterly weep and say,
O that mine eyes were a fountain of tears
that I might weep day and night;
that with Magdalene I may hear Thee say,

Thy sins be forgiven thee,
and with her may love much,
for many sins, yea manifold,
have been forgiven me.
And Thou, All-holy, Good, and
Life-giving Spirit,
despise me not, Thy breath,
despise not Thine own holy things;
but turn Thee again, O Lord, at the last,
and be gracious unto Thy servant.

Commendation

Blessed art Thou, O Lord,
our God,
the God of our Fathers;
who turnest the shadow of death into
the morning;
and lightenest the face of the earth;
who separatest darkness from the face of the light;
and banishest night and bringest back the day;
who lightenest mine eyes,
that I sleep not in death;
who deliverest me from the terror by night,
from the pestilence that walketh in darkness;
who drivest sleep from mine eyes,
and slumber from mine eyelids;
who makest the outgoings of the
morning and evening

to praise Thee;
because I laid me down and slept and
rose up again,
for the Lord sustained me;
because I waked and beheld,
and my sleep was sweet unto me.
Blot out as a thick cloud my transgressions,
and as a cloud my sins;
grant me to be a child of light, a child of the day,
to walk soberly, holily, honestly, as in the day;
vouchsafe to keep me this day without sin.
Thou who upholdest the falling and
liftest the fallen,
let me not harden my heart in provocation,
or temptation of deceitfulness of any sin.
Moreover, deliver me today
from the snare of the hunter
and from the noisome pestilence;
from the arrow that flieth by day,
from the sickness that destroyeth in the
noon day.
Defend this day against my evil,
against the evil of this day defend Thou me.
Let not my days be spent in vanity,
nor my years in sorrow.
One day telleth another,
and one night certifieth another.
O let me hear Thy loving-kindness
betimes in the morning,

for in Thee is my trust;
shew Thou me the way that I should walk in,
for I lift up my soul unto Thee.
Deliver me, O Lord, from mine enemies,
for I flee unto Thee.
Teach me to do the thing that pleaseth Thee,
for Thou art my God;
Let Thy loving Spirit lead me forth
into the land of righteousness.
Quicken me, O Lord, for Thy Name's sake,
and for Thy righteousness' sake
bring my soul out of trouble;
remove from me foolish imaginations,
inspire those which are good
and pleasing in Thy sight.
Turn away mine eyes
lest they behold vanity;
let mine eyes look right on,
and let mine eyelids look straight before me.
Hedge up mine ears with thorns
lest they incline to undisciplined words.
Give me early the ear to hear,
and open mine ears to the instruction
of Thy oracles.
Set a watch, O Lord, before my mouth,
and keep the door of my lips.
Let my word be seasoned with salt,
that it may minister grace to the hearers.
Let no deed be grief unto me

nor offense of heart.
Let me do some work
for which Thou wilt remember me, Lord,
for good,
and spare me according to the greatness
of Thy mercy.
Into Thine hands I commend
my spirit, soul, and body,
which Thou hast created, redeemed, regenerated,
O Lord, Thou God of truth;
and together with me
all mine and all that belongs to me.
Thou hast vouchsafed them to me,
Lord, in Thy goodness.
Guard us from all evil,
guard our souls,
I beseech Thee, O Lord.
Guard us without falling,
and place us immaculate
in the presence of Thy glory
in that day.
Guard my going out and my coming in
henceforth and forever.
Prosper, I pray Thee, Thy servant this day,
and grant him mercy
in the sight of those who meet him.
O God, make speed to save me,
O Lord, make haste to help me.
O turn Thee then unto me,

and have mercy upon me;
give Thy strength unto Thy servant,
and help the son of Thine handmaid.
Shew some token upon me for good,
that they who hate me may see it and be ashamed,
because Thou, Lord, hast holpen me
and comforted me.

MORNING PRAYER

O Thou that hearest the prayer,
unto Thee shall all flesh come.
At evening, and morning, and at noon day,
will I pray and that instantly,
and Thou shalt hear my voice.
My voice shalt Thou hear betimes, O Lord:
early in the morning
will I direct my prayer unto Thee,
and will look up.
Let my prayer be set forth
in Thy sight as the incense.
I have remembered Thee in my bed,
and thought upon Thee when I was waking,
because Thou hast been my Helper.
I yield Thee thanks, Almighty Lord,
everlasting God,
for that Thou hast vouchsafed
to preserve me this night,
not according to my deserts,

but according to Thy holy compassion.
Grant unto me, O Lord,
so to pass this day in Thy holy service,
that the submission of my obedience
may be acceptable unto Thee.
I lift up both heart and hands to the Lord
in the heavens.
Behold, even as the eyes of servants
look unto the hand of their masters,
and as the eyes of a maiden
unto the hand of her mistress,
even so our eyes wait upon the Lord our God,
until He have mercy upon us.
Look Thou upon me, and be merciful unto me,
as Thou usest to do unto those that love
Thy Name.
Give Thy Angels charge over me,
to keep me in all my ways.
Shew me Thy ways, O Lord;
and teach me Thy paths.
Order my steps in Thy word,
and so shall no wickedness have dominion
over me.
Hold Thou up my goings in Thy paths,
that my footsteps slip not.
Put into my mouth words that are honest
and well chosen,
that my conversation and looks,
and my gestures, and all my works,
may be pleasing unto all men that see

and hear me;
that I may find grace in all my speeches
and petitions.

PRAYER OF PENITENCE

O Thou Lover of men,
Thou that art very pitiful:
the Father of mercies,
that art rich in mercy to all that call upon Thee,
I have sinned against Heaven and in Thy sight,
and am no more worthy to be called Thy son,
nor to be made one of Thy hired servants,
no not the lowest.
But I repent;
woe is me! I repent;
help Thou mine impenitence;
and if there be any comfort of love,
by Thy bowels and mercies,
by the multitude, by the riches, of Thy Grace,
by Thy abundant mercy,
by the great love wherewith Thou hast loved us,
be merciful to me a sinner,
be merciful to me of all sinners the greatest,
the most wretched.
Deep calleth unto deep,
the deep of our misery,
unto the deep of Thy compassion;
where sin hath abounded,
there let grace much more abound;

overcome our evil with Thy good;
let mercy rejoice against judgment.

But beyond and before all things,
I believe that Thou art the Christ,
the Son of the Living God;
Thou that didst come into the world to save
sinners,
of whom I am chief,
save me.
Thou that didst come to redeem the lost,
let not one whom Thou hast redeemed, perish.
[Preserve me]
from the recollection of evil things,
that what I have seen and heard
from the wicked, in this world,
I may not remember,
nor ever tell to others;
that I may hate every evil way.
I have deserved death;
but yet I appeal from the tribunal of Thy justice
to the throne of Thy grace.

A MORNING HYMN OF VERY ANCIENT USAGE IN THE CHURCH

Glory be to God on high,
on earth peace,
good-will toward men.

We praise Thee,
   we bless Thee,
   we worship Thee,
   we glorify Thee,
   we give thanks to Thee,
   for Thy great glory,
O Lord God, heavenly King,
   God, the Father Almighty,
   Lord, the Only-begotten Son,
   Jesu Christ,
   and Holy Ghost.
Lord God,
   Lamb of God,
   Son of the Father,
that takest away the sins of the world,
   have mercy upon us.
Thou that takest away the sins of the world,
                     receive our prayer.
Thou that sittest at the right hand of the Father,
                     have mercy upon us.
   For Thou only art Holy,
      Thou only art the Lord,
      Jesus Christ,
      with the Holy Ghost,
   in the Glory of God the Father. Amen.

Evening Prayers

ORDER OF EVENING PRAYER

Meditation

The day is gone,
and I give Thee thanks, O Lord.
Evening is at hand,
make it bright unto us.
As day has its evening
so also has life;
the even of life is age,
age has overtaken me,
make it bright unto us.
Cast me not away in the time of age;
forsake me not when my strength faileth me.
Even to my old age be Thou He,
and even to hoar hairs carry me;
do Thou make, do Thou bear,
do Thou carry and deliver me.
Abide with me, Lord,
for it is toward evening,
and the day is far spent
of this fretful life.
Let Thy strength be made perfect
in my weakness.

Day is fled and gone,
life too is going,
this lifeless life.
Night cometh,
and cometh death,
the deathless death.
Near as is the end of day,
so too the end of life:
we then, also remembering it,
beseech of Thee
for the close of our life,
that Thou wouldest direct it in peace,
Christian, acceptable,
sinless, shameless,
and, if it please Thee, painless,
Lord, O Lord,
gathering us together
under the feet of Thine Elect,
when Thou wilt, and as Thou wilt,
only without shame and sins.
Remember we the days of darkness,
for they shall be many,
lest we be cast into outer darkness.
Remember we to outstrip the night
doing some good thing.
Near is judgment;—
a good and acceptable answer
at the dreadful and fearful judgment seat
of Jesus Christ,
vouchsafe to us, O Lord.

By night I lift up my hands in the sanctuary,
and praise the Lord.
The Lord hath granted His loving-kindness
in the daytime;
and in the night season did I sing of Him,
and made my prayer unto the God of my life.
As long as I live will I magnify Thee
on this manner,
and lift up my hands in Thy Name.
Let my prayer be set forth in Thy sight
as the incense,
and let the lifting up of my hands
be an evening sacrifice.
Blessed art Thou, O Lord, our God,
the God of our fathers,
who hast created the changes of days and nights,
who givest songs in the night,
who hast delivered us from the evil of this day,
who hast not cut off like a weaver my life,
nor from day even to night made an end of me.

Confession

Lord,
as we add day to day
so sin to sin.
The just falleth seven times a day;
and I, an exceeding sinner,
seventy times seven;
wonderful, a horrible thing, O Lord.

But I turn with groans
from my evil ways,
and I return into my heart,
and with all my heart I turn to Thee,
O God of penitents and Saviour of sinners;
and evening by evening I will return
in the innermost marrow of my soul;
and my soul out of the deep
crieth unto Thee.
I have sinned, O Lord, against Thee,
heavily against Thee;
alas, alas, woe is me! for my misery.
I repent, O me! I repent, spare me, O Lord,
I repent, O me, I repent,
help Thou my impenitence.
Be appeased, spare me, O Lord;
be appeased, have mercy on me;
I said, Lord, have mercy upon me,
heal my soul, for I have sinned against
Thee.
Have mercy upon me, O Lord,
after Thy great goodness,
according to the multitude of Thy mercies
do away mine offenses.
Remit the guilt,
heal the wound,
blot out the stains,
clear away the shame,
rescue from the tyranny,
and make me not a public example.

O bring Thou me out of my trouble,
cleanse Thou me from secret fault,
keep back Thy servant also from
presumptuous sins.
My wanderings of mind
and idle talking
lay not to my charge.
Remove the dark and muddy flood
of foul and wicked thoughts.
O Lord,
I have destroyed myself;
whatever I have done amiss, pardon mercifully.
Deal not with us after our sins,
neither reward us after our iniquities.
Look mercifully upon our infirmities;
and for the glory of Thy All-holy Name,
turn from us all those ills and miseries,
which by our sins, and by us through them,
are most righteously and worthily deserved.

Commendation

To my weariness, O Lord,
vouchsafe Thy rest,
to my exhaustion
renew Thy strength.
Lighten mine eyes that I sleep not in death.
Deliver me from the terror by night,
the pestilence that walketh in darkness.
Supply me with healthy sleep,

and to pass through this night without fear.
O keeper of Israel,
who neither slumberest nor sleepest,
guard me this night from all evil,
guard my soul, O Lord.
Visit me with the visitation of Thine own,
reveal to me wisdom in the visions of the night.
If not, for I am not worthy, not worthy,
at least, O loving Lord,
let sleep be to me a breathing time
as from toil, so from sin.
Yea, O Lord,
nor let me in my dreams imagine
what may anger Thee,
what may defile me.
Let not my loins be filled with illusions,
yea, let my reins chasten me in the night season,
yet without grievous terror.
Preserve me from the black sleep of sin;
all earthly and evil thoughts
put to sleep within me.
Grant to me light sleep,
rid of all imaginations
fleshly and satanical.
Lord, Thou knowest
how sleepless are mine unseen foes,
and how feeble my wretched flesh,
who madest me;
shelter me with the wing of Thy pity;

awaken me at the fitting time,
the time of prayer;
and give me to seek Thee early,
for Thy glory, and for Thy service.

Into Thy hands, O Lord, I commend myself,
my spirit, soul, and body:
Thou didst make, and didst redeem them;
and together with me, all my friends
and all that belongs to me.
Thou hast vouchsafed them to me, Lord,
in Thy goodness.
Guard my lying down and my rising up,
from henceforth and forever.
Let me remember Thee on my bed,
and search out my spirit;
let me wake up and be present with Thee;
let me lay down in peace, and take my rest:
for it is Thou, Lord, only
that makest me dwell in safety.

WARNINGS AND
PREPARATORY MEDITATIONS
IN THE EVENING,
RAISING OF THE MIND
TOWARD GOD

In war there is the note of charge, fitted for the onset;

of recall, whereby stragglers are recalled:

So the mind of man, as it must be excited in the morning, so in the evening, as by a note of recall, is it to be called back to itself and its Leader,

by
{
  a scrutiny and inquisition or examination of self;
  thanksgivings.
}

1. Scrutiny and Inquisition; an Examination.

A good man would rather know his infirmity, than the foundations of the earth, or the heights of the heavens. (S. Aug.)

But that knowledge of our own infirmity is not attained but by diligent inquisition: without which the mind is for the most part blind, and sees nothing of that which pertains to it.

There are many hiding places and recesses in the mind, etc. (Cicero)

You must come to the knowledge of, before you can amend, yourself.

An unknown sin grows worse and worse (Seneca), and is deprived of cure.

The heart is deceitful above all things.

The old man is bound up in a thousand folds.

Therefore take care of thyself.

Points chiefly to be inquired.

What hast thou today { that {
done, said,
read, written,
befits a Christian, a priest, father, etc.
may confirm faith, obedience,
increase knowledge, the good government of mind, body,
work out the salvation of thyself, others.

We see that God Himself concluded each day of the old creation in no other manner than by an examination of the works of each.

And He beheld that all were good.

Cato exacted from himself an account of every day's business, and also Pythagoras. (Cicero)

Ausonius from Pythagoras:

Nor let sweet sleep upon thine eyes descend,

Till thou hast judged its deeds at each day's
end.

King David, when the day was over, meditated,
and searched out his spirit.

In this Areopagetic nightly examination,
beware that thou shew thyself the judge,
not the patron, of thy sins:
and say in the tribunal of thy mind,
say with grief and indignation,
who will set scourges over my thoughts,
and the discipline of wisdom over my heart?
(Eccles. xxiii. 2)

If we judged ourselves, we should not be
judged.

Prayer is the guardian of the sleeping,
the confidence of the waking.
(S. Greg. Nyss.)

And we think him not safe who is unde-
fended by the arms and the guard of
prayer.

Rightly therefore teacheth Rabbi J[archi?]
that penitence must not be procrastinated
till the morrow.

Behold the hope of advantage and eternal
salvation shall have deceived itself forever,
unless even in this very night thou shalt
have freed thy soul.

And if an examination of this kind takes place
for some days, or, at farthest, one month, with

penitence, it may suffice to form a perfect habit
of virtue.

AN EVENING HYMN

O joyful Light of the holy glory
of the Father, Immortal, Heavenly, Holy, Blessed,
Jesus Christ:
beholding the evening light
we glorify the Father, and the Son, and the
Holy Spirit of God.
Worthy art Thou in all seasons
to be hymned with sacred voices,
Son of God,
Giver of hope;
wherefore the world glorifieth Thee.

INTRODUCTION TO THE
EVENING SACRIFICE

Let me be mindful of Thy Name,
O Lord, in the night,
and keep Thy law.
Let our evening prayer ascend to Thee,
and Thy mercy descend to us;
Thou that givest songs in the night;
that makest the outgoings of the morning
and evening to praise Thee;
that givest to Thy beloved the sleep of health.

Confessional Prayers

INTRODUCTION TO CONFESSION

Two things I recognize, O Lord, in myself:
nature, which Thou hast made;
sin, which I have added.
I confess, that by sin I have depraved nature;
but call to remembrance, that I am a wind
that passeth away,
and returneth not again;
for of myself I cannot return again from sin.
Take away from me that which I have made;
let that which Thou hast made remain in me;
that the price of Thy precious Blood perish not!
Let not my wickedness destroy
what Thy goodness hath redeemed.
O Lord my God, if I have so done
as to become Thy culprit,
can I have so done as no longer
to be Thy servant?
If I have thence destroyed my innocence,
have I at all thence destroyed Thy mercy?
If I have committed that for which
Thou mightest condemn me,
hast Thou at all lost that by which
Thou art wont to save?

Truth, Lord: my conscience
meriteth damnation,
but no offense equals Thy compassion.
Spare me therefore;
because it is not unbefitting Thy justice,
nor unwonted to Thy mercy,
nor difficult to Thy power,
to spare the penitent.
Thou who hast created me,
do not destroy me;
Thou who hast created me,
do not condemn me.
Thou who hast created me
by Thy goodness,
let not Thy work come to nought
through my iniquity.
What is Thine in me, acknowledge;
what is mine, take away.
Look on me, the wretched,
O boundless Loving-kindness:
on me, the wicked,
O Compassion that extendest to all!
Infirm I come to the Almighty,
wounded I hasten to the Physician:
reserve for me the gentleness
of Thy compassion,
who hast so long held suspended the sword
of Thy vengeance.
Blot out the number of my crimes,
renew the multitude of Thy compassions.

However unclean, Thou canst cleanse me;
however blind, enlighten me;
however weak, restore me;
yea, though dead, raise me.
Of what kind soever I am, be it good or bad,
I am ever Thine.
If Thou cast me out, who shall take me in?
If Thou disregard me, who shall look on me?
More canst Thou remit, than I commit;
more canst Thou spare, than I offend.
Let not noxious pleasures overcome me;
at the least let not any perverse habit
overwhelm me;
[preserve me]
from depraved and lawless desires;
from vain, hurtful, impure imaginations;
from the illusions of evil spirits;
from pollutions of soul and of body.

AN ACT OF CONFESSION

I have sinned;
of a verity, O Lord, and I am made
of sins; for even my life maketh it manifest.
I confess it unto Thee, seeing that if I would,
I could not conceal it from Thee, O Lord.
Who can bring a clean thing out of an
unclean?
I am a sinner, of unclean seed,

of an unclean womb.
My mother conceived me in sin;
 a root of bitterness,
  a shoot of a wild olive tree.
I have sinned with my fathers; I have done
 amiss and dealt wickedly, (Ps. cvi 6)
I have done perversely, I have committed
 wickedness: (1 Kings viii. 47)
I have borne myself forwardly in the
 covenant;
I have cast away the law: (Isa. v. 24)
rejected discipline; (Prov. xv. 32)
vexed Thy Holy Spirit; (Isa. lxiii. 10)
done the imaginations of my heart:
      (Jer. xviii. 12)
gone on from sin to sin;
have not feared Thee;
have not returned; (Luke xv. 18)
not even when recalled; (Jer. v. 13)
nor when afflicted; (Jer. v. 13; Prov. xxiii. 35)
but have hardened my heart; (Heb. iii. 13)
provoked Thee; (1 Kings xvi. 33)
and all this Thou hast seen; (Lam. iii. 59)
and held Thy peace. (Ps. l. 21)

AN ACT OF CONFESSION

God, Thou knowest my foolishness,
 and my faults are not hid from Thee.

I also acknowledge them, and my sin is ever
before me.
I have not covered my transgressions, like Adam.
(Job xxxi. 33)
I incline not my heart to any evil thing,
(Ps. cxli. 4)
but I will acknowledge my sin unto Thee,
(Ps. xxxii. 5)
and all that is within me; (Ps. ciii. 1)
and all my bones shall say, (Ps. xxxv. 10)
I have sinned:
I have gone astray, like a sheep that is lost;
as a bullock unaccustomed to the yoke;
(Jer. xxxi. 18)
I have returned like a dog to his vomit;
as a sow that was washed, to her wallowing
in the mire.
I give glory to the Lord God of Israel, saying,
I have sinned; and thus and thus have I done.
Break not the bruised reed;
quench not the smoking flax;
let not the waterflood drown me,
neither let the deep swallow me up,
and let not the pit shut her mouth upon me.
Lord, Thou knowest all my desire,
and my groaning is not hid from Thee.
Thou knowest, Lord, that I speak the
truth in Christ, and lie not,
my conscience also bearing me witness
in the Holy Ghost,

that I have great heaviness and continual sorrow
in my heart,
because I have thus sinned against Thee;
that I am a burden to myself, in that I cannot
sorrow more;
that I beseech from Thee
a contrite heart,
groanings that cannot be uttered,
tears of blood.
Woe is me! for my dryness,
for the hardness of my heart,
for the dryness of my eyes.
Lord, I repent; I repent, O Lord!
help Thou mine impenitence;
and more and more bruise, and wound, and
pierce, and strike my heart.
Behold, O Lord,
that I am indignant with myself
on account of the foolish and vain and
mischievous and dangerous desires of my flesh:
that I abhor myself
for the madness and baseness and vileness of those
desires,
worthy of confusion and reproach;
that all the day long my confusion is before me,
and the shame of my face hath covered me.
Woe is me!
that I did not reverence nor dread
the incomprehensibleness of the Glory,
the tremendous Power,

the awfulness of the Presence,
the exquisite Justice,
the admirable Goodness.
How have I been drawn away by mine own
lusts!
how have I hated reproof!
and have not obeyed the voice of my
teachers!
Behold, O Lord,
that fearfulness and trembling are come upon
me,
and the fear of death hath fallen upon me!
What fear, what terror, what trembling,
what agony, what extremity have I yet to see!
What confusion will seize me!
What shades will surround me!
How terrible is Thy judgment seat, O God!
when the thrones are set and the Angels in
presence,
and men brought in and the books opened,
and the works investigated,
and the thoughts scrutinized,
and the hidden things of darkness made
known:
what will be the judgment against me?
when there is the incorruptible Judge,
and the tremendous Tribunal,
and the excuseless defense,
and the irrefragable accusation,

and the fearful punishment, and the eternal
                    Gehenna,
and the pitiless Angels, and the open hell-mouth,
and the roaring river of fire,
and the prison of darkness, and that darkness
                    rayless,
and the bed of live coals, and the restless worm,
and the indissoluble chains, and the immeasurable
                    chaos,
and the gulf that cannot be passed, and the lament
            that cannot be consoled,
    and none to assist, to advocate, to free!

        Behold, O Lord,
    I adjudge myself worthy of, and amenable to,
                    and guilty of,
        eternal punishment;
    yea, and of all the straits of this world.
From Thee, O Lord, I have merited death, from
            Thee, the Just One;
but yet to Thee, O Lord, I appeal, to Thee, the
            Merciful One;
    from the tribunal of justice, to the mercy seat
                of grace;
        permit, O Lord, this appeal:
    if Thou dost not, we perish!
        And, O Lord, carest Thou not that we
                    perish?
    Thou who wilt have all men to be saved,
        who art not willing that any should perish?

Behold me, O Lord,
  condemned by my own judgment!
Behold me; and enter not Thou, O Lord, into
        judgment with Thy servant!
I am less than the least of all Thy mercies;
I am not worthy to be lowest of Thine hired
        servants;
I am not worthy to gather the crumbs that fall
        from Thy table;
I am not worthy to touch the hem of Thy
        garment.
    And now, O Lord, humbling myself under
        Thy mighty hand,
  I bend my knees to Thee, and fall down to the
        ground, on my face.
    I stretch forth my hands unto Thee;
  my soul gaspeth unto Thee as a thirsty land.
      I dare not so much as to lift up
          mine eyes unto heaven,
  but I smite upon my breast.
      Out of the deep hath my soul cried unto
Thee, and all that is within me;
for Thy great mercy, and for the multitude of
        Thy loving-kindnesses,
    for Thy Name's sake, for the glory of Thy
        Name,
        be merciful to my sin:
    for it is great; for it is exceedingly great.
For the multitude, the great multitude, the riches,
        the abundance,

the superabundance of Thy
loving-kindnesses,
be merciful unto me, O Lord, a sinner:
Lord, O Lord, be merciful unto me, of sinners
the greatest.
Lord, let Thy mercy rejoice against Thy
justice, in my sin.
O my Lord, where sin hath abounded, there
let Grace more exceedingly abound.
O Lord, hear: O Lord, forgive; O Lord, hearken,
and do;
defer not for Thine own sake, O my God!

A CONFESSION OF FAITH

I believe that, for a great mystery of godliness;
for us men, and for our salvation,
Jesus the Man,
the Son of the Father, the Anointed of the
Spirit,
our Lord, both as Creator and Redeemer,
was God manifest in the flesh;
that He worketh efficaciously and manifestly,
by illumination of science, and infusion of grace,
in reprehension, and teaching, and long-suffering,
and assistance, and witnessing, and consolation:
the gifts and graces of the Spirit.

A PRAYER FOR GRACE

[Give me grace] unceasingly to return thanks
 to Thy word and only Son:
  as the Purifier of our nature, in His
    conception and nativity;
  the Liberator of our persons, in His passion,
    cross, and death;
  the Victor over hell, in His descent,
   over death, in His resurrection;
 our Precursor, in His ascension;
 our Advocate, in His session;
 the Restorer of our faith, in His second advent:
  Who to our destroyer opposes Himself
    as our Saviour,
  to Abaddon, as Jesus;
  to Satan, the adversary, as our Mediator;
  to the devil, the calumniator, as our
    Advocate;
  to the accuser, as our Intercessor;
  to him that leadeth us captive, as our
    Redeemer.

AN ACT OF INTERCESSION

[Grant] that Christ Himself may be formed in us,
 that we may be made comformable to His
    image;

that when I am lukewarm in prayer, and stand in
need of any grace,
or of celestial consolation,
I may remember Thy session of Intercession,
and of return to judgment;
when I am inflamed by passion and evil
concupiscience,
I may bear in mind Thy tremendous and fearful
tribunal,
and that the last trumpet may ceaselessly
sound in mine ears.
That for the sake of Thine Anointed,
I may receive, O Father who anointest, Thine
anointing,
the grace that bringeth salvation, Thy
ineffable
gift of the Holy Spirit,
in healthful compunction, and clearness of
knowledge,
fervent prayer and diffusion of charity,
the witness of the Seal and the Earnest;
that I may never extinguish the Spirit,
nor strive against Him, nor grieve Him, nor
ever insult Him, O Lord.
That we may be called in Thy Church,
and being lively members thereof in wish and
will, as it is Catholic,
we may be partakers in the communion,
as it is holy,
of holy persons and holy things,

of holy prayers and the holy liturgy,
to a trust in the remission of sins,
    and hope of resurrection and translation unto
        life eternal.
Lord, increase my faith as a grain of mustard
        seed!
    Let it not be dead, nor temporary, nor
        hypocritical;
    but let it operate through charity, co-operate
    with works, be the supplier of virtue,
    conquer the world, and be most holy.

O God of truth, the Prince of peace,
    let there be peace and truth in our days;
    let the multitude of them that believe be of one
        heart and of one soul.
O Thou that dost not break the bruised reed,
    nor quench the smoking flax,
    establish all them that stand in truth and grace,
    restore them that are falling through error
        or sin.
I beseech Thee, O Lord, of Thy mercy,
    let Thine anger be turned away from this city,
        and from this house,
    for we have sinned against Thee.

Be Thou pleased favorably to regard this place
        and all this land,
    tempering justice with mercy.
Grant that I may love them that love me, though

I know them not;
and bring them, as me, into Thy heavenly
kingdom,
and grant that I may shew them the mercy of
God,
[by remembering them] in my prayers;
that I, with those for whom I have prayed,
and those for whom I am in any way soever
bound to pray,
and with all the people of God,
may have an entrance into Thy kingdom;
there to appear in righteousness, and to be
satisfied with glory.

Blessed is the people, O Lord, that can rejoice in
Thee;
they shall walk in the light of Thy
countenance;
their delight shall be daily, O Lord, in Thy
Name;
in Thy glory shall they make their boast.
My mouth shall speak the praise of the Lord,
and let all flesh bless His Holy Name forever.
O magnify the Lord with me;
and let us exalt His Name together!
Hearken unto me, ye that fear God;
and I will tell you what He hath done for
my soul.
Be Thou exalted, O God, above the heavens;

and Thy glory above all the earth.
I will give thanks unto Thee, O Lord, with my
whole heart,
in the assembly of the righteous, and in the
congregation.
Open my mouth, that I may bless Thy Name;
set me free from all things else for the telling of
Thy praise;
I will sing unto Thee in the sight of the
Angels.
Accept the praises, which I desire to offer,
an unworthy sinner, verily unworthy:
but yet I would fain they may be devoted
and grateful to Thee!
Thou art worthy, Lord God, to receive them;
Thou art my God, and I will praise and exalt
Thee:
I will sing unto the Lord as long as I live;
I will praise my God while I have any being.
Glory to God in the highest:
on earth peace; good-will toward men!
Glory and blessing, virtue and power,
honor and thanksgiving, riches and holiness,
praise and wisdom, power and salvation,
be to our God That liveth forever,
that sitteth upon the throne, and to the Lamb
that was slain.
Amen: Hallelujah!
Hosanna in the highest: blessed be He that
cometh in the Name of the Lord!

AN ACT OF CONFESSION

Behold me, O Lord, behold me; the greatest, the
worst, the most wretched of sinners. And what
shall I now say, or in what shall I open my
mouth? What shall I answer, when I am guilty,
guilty, guilty! I will go over my sins unto Thee
in the bitterness of my soul; O that it may be
in its bitterest bitterness! Behold, for my peace
I had great bitterness. O Lord, by these things
men live, and in all these things is the life of my
spirit: so wilt Thou recover me, and make me
to live. Like a crane or a swallow, so will I lament; I will mourn as a dove. I beseech Thee,
O Lord, by all Thy mercy, let Thy most
righteous indignation and fury be turned away
from me, because I have sinned, and that grievously. I have sinned against Thee, most often
and grievously, I have sinned against Thee!

O Father of mercies, I beseech Thy fatherly loving-kindness, despise not an unclean worm, a
dead dog, a putrid corpse; despise not me! Yea
rather regard me, O Lord, regard me with
those eyes wherewith Thou didst regard Magdalene in the banquet, Peter in the hall, the thief
on the cross; that with Peter I may weep, with
the thief may confess, with Magdalene may
love; may love much, yea very much, for that
many sins are forgiven me. Spare me, O Lord;

spare me, a penitent: at the least desiring to be a penitent, and preparing thereto; recollecting my sins with bitterness, indignant with myself concerning them, remembering and laying hold of Thy most bitter passion. Spare, O Lord, have mercy! Spare me, O Lord, have mercy on me! pity me, because it is not difficult to Thy power, nor unbefitting Thy justice, nor unusual to Thy clemency.

That I should thus, for leeks and garlick have left the Bread of Angels! That I should thus, for the husks of swine, have despised my Father's table! Woe wretched, woe frenzied me! Who fascinated me to such madness? O that Thou wouldst reign to receive me again! At least I desire to return: better was it with me then, my state being as it is now. Full therefore of confusion, unworthy to name, or invoke, or think upon Thy Name, were it not for Thine innate goodness: yet, relying on that very goodness, supplicant, humble, prostrate, I return to Thee; nor ask I for any thing, but that which Thou hast bestowed most often, and bestowest most willingly; that, which unless Thou wert again and again to bestow, flesh could not abide, none could stand. Have mercy on me a sinner, the greatest of sinners, and for that very reason needing the greatest mercy. And Thy mercy is the greatest: it reacheth to the Heaven above, it freeth from the lowest hell; it is marvelous. Magnify Thy mercy to me; if Thou seekest to glorify it infinitely, extend it to me; at no time, in no place, hath it been, will it be, more glorious in the pardon of a sinner. If Thou willest, Lord, that I should leave Thee, give me another Thyself: else I will not give Thee up. Let the Spirit of truth lead me into truth.

To Thee, O Lord, I confess, because if I would, I cannot conceal; to Thee my very many, my very great, my very heinous sins. I profess also to grieve, as Thou knowest. But I need more grief: I plainly need it. I am far from that which I ought to have. I can sin much; I cannot repent much. My dryness! my dryness! woe unto me! I cannot much: I would much. I know that much is not enough. Would that I had such grief, or even more! But of myself I cannot obtain it. I am parched, I am parched like a potsherd. Woe is me! Thou, O Lord, increase the fountain of tears that I have; supply that I have not: give me a molten heart, unutterable groans! Meanwhile, since my mind is willing, accept me according to that I have, not according to that I have not. I will extend it, since I cannot increase it, through all the years of my life.

After so many backslidings, with what confidence can I now return? With none. Altogether confused, altogether covered with con-

fusion, I sit, I walk, I lie down. Nor should I
dare to do it, nor could I do aught but despair,
and act like the desperate, unless there were
yet a hope left. And what hope? That thou
wilt extend Thy mercy to seventy times seven.
That measure of forgiveness Thou hast enjoined to us. Hast Thou enjoined this to us, and
wilt not Thou Thyself practice the same? Yea
and much more. That be far from Thee, that
Thou shouldst require more perfection in us
than existeth in Thyself: that we must forgive
until seventy times seven but Thou wilt not
forgive. For Thy mercy surpasseth ours, as far
as Thyself surpasseth us. I then, trusting in Thy
mercy, that forgiveth at the least seventy times
seven, stand afar off; and lowlily, as I ought,
and most humbly striking my breast, say and
repeat, again and again, God have mercy on me
a sinner, on me a most wretched sinner, on me
the chief of sinners, on me who am altogether
sin, on me, who am a very hyperbole of sin,
O Thou to whom prayer can never be made
without a hope of pardon.

Shall God forgive, and thou not repent? God forbid! I do in a sort repent: I fear me not suf-
ficiently. I would that it were more: I should
rejoice, were it more: I grieve that it is no
more. For I wish that I could more, and grieve
that I can no more. I confess that my very grief
is to be lamented; and I grieve that it is thus to

be lamented. And who will give me to lament it more? I would do so, were it in my power: but it is not. It is in my power to know that I ought; to wish that I did; to will is present with me; but how to perform that which is good, I find not.

Do Thou, O Lord, give me power: if Thou wilt, Thou canst: Thou canst turn even the hard rock into a pool. Give tears: give a fountain of waters to my head. Give the grace of tears. Drop down, ye heavens, from above, and bedew the dryness of my heart. Give me, O Lord, this grace. None were more welcome to me; neither riches, nor all the good things of this world were to be coveted in comparison of tears: tears, such as Thou didst give David of old, or Jeremiah, Saint Peter, or Saint Mary Magdalene. At least give me a dropping eye: let me not altogether be a flint. If I may not water my couch, nor wash Thy feet: if I may not weep bitterly as Peter, plentifully as Jeremiah (and yet, O that it might be even thus!), at least one or two little tears, which Thou mayest put into Thy bottle, and write in Thy book. But if I cannot gain this much, woe is me! I ame like a pumice, like very lime, fervent in cold water. Careless of my state where I least ought to be so; without feeling. Mourning enough, when there is no occasion: cold, arid, dead, where there is the greatest.

At least give me of the tears of Christ, which He
shed plentifully in the days of His flesh. Bestow on me from that store: in Him there is
superfluity for my deficiency.

A SHORT PRAYER AFTER
CONFESSION

O my Saviour Christ, Christ my Saviour! who
will grant that I may die rather than again offend Thee? Christ my Saviour, O my Saviour!
Lord, let a new manner of life prove that a new
spirit hath descended on me: for true penitence
is new life; and true praise unremitted penitence, and the observation of a perpetual sabbath from sin, its occasions, fuel, and danger.
For as penitence destroys old sins, so do new
sins destroy penitence.

O God, my heart is ready;
   so saith the Psalmist:
      but I fear, Lord, lest mine should not be
      ready.
  I would that it were: I grieve, if it be not.
Lord, prepare it: assist my disposal, and supply
      my preparation of it.
  I will put my sins before my sight;
   that they may not be put before Thine.

Prayers of Deprecation

A DEPRECATION

O Lord, Thou knowest, and canst, and willest
the good of my soul.
Miserable man am I;
I neither know, nor can, nor, as I ought,
will it.
Thou, O Lord, I beseech Thee,
in Thine ineffable affection,
so order concerning me,
and so dispose,
as Thou knowest to be most pleasing to Thee,
and most good for me.
[Thine is]
goodness, grace;
love, kindness;
benignity, gentleness, consideration;
forbearance, long-suffering;
much pity, great pity;
mercies, multitude of mercies,
yearning of mercies;
kind yearnings, deep yearnings;
in passing over,
in overlooking, in disregarding;
many seasons, many years;

[punishing] unwillingly, not willingly;
not to the full,
not correspondently,
in wrath remembering mercy,
repenting of the evil,
compensating doubly,
ready to pardon,
to be reconciled,
to be appeased.

A LITANY OF DEPRECATION

Father, the Creator,
Son, the Redeemer,
Spirit, the Regenerator,
destroy me not,
whom Thou hast created, redeemed, regenerated.
Remember not, Lord, my sins,
nor the sins of my forefathers;
neither take vengeance for our sins, theirs,
nor mine.
Spare us, Lord, them and me,
spare Thy people,
and, among Thy people, Thy servant,
who is redeemed with Thy precious Blood;
and be not angry with us forever.
Be merciful, be merciful; spare us, Lord,
and be not angry with us forever.
Be merciful, be merciful; have pity on us, Lord

and be not angry with us to the full.
Deal not, O Lord,
deal not with me after mine iniquities,
neither recompense me according to my sins;
but after Thy great pity,
deal with me,
and according to the multitude of Thy mercies,
recompense me;
after that so great pity,
and that multitude of mercies,
as Thou didst to our fathers
in the times of old;—
by all that is dear unto Thee.
From all evil and adversity,
in all time of need;
from this evil and this adversity,
in this time;
raise me, rescue me, save me, O Lord.
Deliver me, O Lord,
and destroy me not.
On the bed of sickness;
in the hour of death;
in the day of judgment,
in that dreadful and fearful day,
rescue me, Lord, and save me;—
from seeing the Judge's face overcast,
from being placed on the left,
from hearing the dreadful word,
"Depart from Me,"
from being bound in chains of darkness,

from being cast into the outer darkness,
from being tormented in the pit of fire
and brimstone,
where the smoke of the torments
ascendeth forever.
Be merciful, be merciful,
spare us, pity us,
O Lord:
and destroy us not forever,
deliver and save us.
Let it not be, O Lord; and that it be not,
take away from me, O Lord,
hardness of heart,
desperateness after sinning,
blindness of heart,
contempt of Thy threats,
a cauterized conscience,
a reprobate mind,
the sin against the Holy Ghost,
the sin unto death,
the four crying sins;
the six which forerun
the sin against the Holy Ghost.
Deliver me
from all ills and abominations of this world,
from plague, famine, and war;
earthquake, flood, and fire,
the stroke of immoderate rain and drought,
blast and blight;
thunder, lightning and tempest;

epidemic sickness, acute and malignant,
unexpected death;
from ills and difficulties in the Church,
from private interpretation,
from innovation in things sacred,
from heterodox teaching;
from unhealthy inquiries and
interminable disputes,
from heresies, schisms, scandals,
public and private,
from making gods of kings,
from flattering of the people,
from the indifference of Saul,
from the scorn of Michal,
from the greediness of Hophni,
from the plunder of Athaliah,
from the priesthood of Micah,
from the brotherhood of Simon and Judas,
from the doctrine of men unlearned
and unestablished,
from the pride of novices,
from the people resisting the priest:—
from ills and difficulties in the state,
from anarchy, many rulers, tyranny,
from Asher, Jeroboam, Rehoboam,
Gallio, Haman,
the profligacy of Athithophel,
the foolishness of Zoan,   [Isa. xix.]
the statutes of Omri,
the justice of Jezebel,

the overflowings of Belial, [Ps. xviii. 4]
the courage of Peor,
the valley of Achor,
pollution of blood or seed,
incursion of enemies,
civil war,
bereavement of good governors,
accession of evil and unprincipled governors;
from an intolerable life,
in despondence, sickness, ill-fame,
distress, peril, slavery, restlessness:
from death
in sin, shame, tortures,
desperateness, defilement, violence, treachery;
from death unexpected,
from death eternal.

AN ACT OF DEPRECATION

Look down, O Lord our God,
from Thy lofty dwelling-place, and from the
Throne of Thy Glory.
Thou, Who dwellest on high, and beholdest
the humble,
look down upon us, and destroy us not;
yea, rather deliver us from evil.
From all evil and misfortune,
deliver us.

As of old time Thou didst deliver our fathers,
     deliver us.
 By whatsoever is dear to Thee, or beloved
     by Thee,
     deliver us.
   In all our straits,
     deliver us.
 From the evils of the future state,
  from Thine anger,
  but yet more from Thy ceasing to be angry,
from everlasting damnation,
from all the terrors of the life to come,
from the wrathful countenance of the Judge,
from being placed on the left hand,
from the hearing of that dreadful and
     terrible voice,
   Depart from Me,
from being cast into outer darkness,
from eternal chains under darkness,
from the lake of fire and brimstone,
 where the smoke of their torments goeth up
    forever and ever,
    deliver us.
 Spare us, O Lord. Have mercy upon us.
Deliver us; and let us never be confounded.
   From spiritual evils;
 from blindness and hardness of heart,
   which lead to impenitence;
 from softness and from hardness of forehead,
 from a seared conscience,

and ceasing from penitence after sin,
from a reprobate mind,
from contempt of Thy threatenings,
from the sin unto death,
from the sin against the Holy Ghost,
have mercy upon us, and deliver us, O Lord!
That I be not parched among the tares and stubble,
nor grieve among those that are on the left hand,
nor withered by the tempest,
nor lament in the fire that is never quenched,
nor be condemned to the flames,
nor suffer shame in Gehenna,
nor waste away among the overflowings of
Belial,
nor weep in the chains of darkness,
nor gnash the teeth in the banishment of the
reprobate;
being miserable, thrice miserable,
with the fiends in darkness, downward
in the abyss, which even Satan himself dreadeth
and abhorreth.
[On the one hand]
is the vision of God:
[On the other]
the hiding of His face.
It is hard to be separated from the saints;
harder to be severed from God.
It is a thing full of shame to be bound
and cast out,
full of woe to be cast into the fire;

full of sadness to call and not to be heard;
full of bitterness to ask unpitied
for a drop of water, and not to gain it.
Deliver me from all evil and misfortune,
from men of corrupt minds,
from Ashur, (Hos. xi. 5)
from Jeroboam, (1 Kings xii. 26)
from Rehoboam, (1 Kings xii. 13)
from the valley of Achor, (Josh. vii. 25, 26)
from the evil spirit of the men of Shechem,
                                 (Judg. ix. 23)
from every stumbling block, grief, infamy,
from a deceitful tongue,
from perverse lips,
from snares,
from all enemies, visible, invisible,
    corporeal, spiritual,
from vices and sins,
from lusts and temptations,
from the attacks of demons,
from the spirit of fornication,
from the desire of vain glory,
from all uncleanness of soul and body,
from anger and ill will,
from polluted thoughts,
from blindness of heart.
O Thou, Who didst once say to Thy
                destroying Angel,
            It is enough;
        hold now Thine hand.

[Hear me] in my prayers and vows,
my straits and perils,
my infirmities and necessities,
my temptations and tribulations;
repel the concupiscence of gluttony,
give the virtue of abstinence;
chase the spirit of fornication,
give the love of chastity;
extinguish the covetousness of the world,
give poverty of spirit;
restrain headstrong passion,
kindle in me the spirit of gentleness;
remove the sorrow of this world,
increase spiritual joy;
repel boastfulness of mind,
bestow compunction of heart.
Give strength of faith,
security of hope,
the preservation of salvation.
Give contempt of the world.
[Give me a place among those that]
shall enter into joy,
into the joy that is full,
into the joy that no man taketh away;
[That I may have a portion]
on the right hand,
in tranquillity,
in a place of verdure, of dew,
in paradise,

in a land of refreshment,
in Abraham's bosom,
in the tabernacles of the saints;
that being on the right hand of God,
I may be made happy in His rest,
rejoice in His honor,
keep holy day in His eternity,
be glorified by Him that is Thrice-holy,
be blessed among His Angels,
enjoy pleasure in His Light,
[amidst the] Psalms that are above,
[and] the Songs of Heaven.
Give me the girdle, the helmet, the breastplate,
the shield, the sandals, the sword,
above all things prayer.
Grant unto me the power and opportunity
of well doing,
that before the day of my decease I may have
wrought at least somewhat,
whose good fruit may remain;
that I may appear with righteousness,
and be satisfied with glory.
O Thou that didst add fifteen years
to the life of Hezekiah,
grant to me such a space of life,
at least of a sufficient space,
wherein I may be able to bewail my sins;
and, with Thy other blessings, send
(best gift of all) a holy end;

a good and holy end of life,
a glorious and joyful resurrection.
                  Bless our increase
from the fruits of the earth and its fullness;
make peace in our borders;
fill us with the flour of wheat;
satisfy our poor with bread;
make fast the bars of our gates;
bless our children amidst us;
clothe our enemies with confusion;
grant us seasonableness of weather;
bestow on us the fruits of the earth;
repel carnal desires;
restore health to the weak,
to the fallen grant renovation;
to voyagers and travelers
[grant] a prosperous journey and a port of
                              safety;
to the afflicted joy;
to the oppressed ease;
to the captives liberty;
health of mind,
soundness of body.

AN ACT OF DEPRECATION

Cast not Thy servant away in anger,
                                        (Ps. xxvii. 9)
nor hide Thine eyes,

nor cover Thy face, (Job xiii. 24)

nor interpose a cloud,

nor shut Thine ear, (Lam. iii. 8)

nor forsake me, (Ps. xxxvii. 1)

nor leave me forever,

nor despise me, (Ps. xxvii. 9)

nor be silent, (Ps. xxxviii. 13)

nor slumber, (Matt. viii. 24)

nor stand afar off, (Ps. x. 1)

nor repel me, (Ps. xliv. 23)

nor utterly take Thy loving-kindness from
me,   (Ps. lxxxix. 33)

nor falsify Thy truth,

nor rebuke me in Thine indignation,
                              (Ps. vi. 1)

nor chasten me in Thy displeasure,
                              (Ps. xxxviii. 1)

nor cast me away from Thy presence,

nor count me a reprobate from among
Thy children,

nor take Thy Holy Spirit from me,
                              (Ps. lvii. 11)

nor forget me forever, (Ps. lxxiv. 19)

nor be wroth very sore, (Isa. lxiv. 9)

nor shut me up nor consume me in the hand
of mine iniquity, (Ps. xvi. 9; Isa. lxiv. 7)

nor tarry, (Hab. ii. 1)

nor gather my soul with sinners. (Ps. xxvi. 9)

If by Thy permission, we suffer for a while the
power of the enemy,

yet let us not in any wise be swallowed up
    by his insatiable jaws.
Let the lion be conquered by the lamb,
the mighty spirit by feeble flesh.

Prayers of Penitence

OF PENITENCE

CONTRITION: bitterness of soul; compunction of
heart;
   a torn, a broken, a contrite soul;
   sorrow before God: groaning: indignation.
CONFESSION: acknowledgment: prayer
   deprecating the past and the future.
All have sinned;
  If Thou, Lord; . . . who shall abide?
  No flesh shall be justified before Thee.
  He cannot answer one of a thousand.
  What then? whether in vain?
  God hath granted repentance unto life.
                      (Acts xi. 18)
  A place is left for repentance, if sin only lieth
       at the door. (Gen. iv. 7)
  Yet now there is hope concerning this thing.
                       (Ezra x. 2)
  There may be a lengthening. (Dan. v. 27)
  And God solicits
  by proclaiming, (Isa. xlv. 7) complaining,
                      (Jer. viii. 4)
  by oath, (Ezek. xxxiii. 4) by waiting,
                     (Isa. xxx. 18)

promising, if paradise to innocence,
the kingdom of heaven to penitence;
threatening, unless—

(Luke xiii. 5; John viii. 24)

Prayer sacrificeth the mind, conquereth the devil,
pleaseth God.

Fasting sacrificeth the body, conquereth the flesh,
benefiteth ourselves.

Almsgiving sacrificeth the goods, conquereth the
world, benefiteth our neighbor.

SUBJECTS FOR MEDITATION
BEFORE PENITENTIAL
PRAYERS

Thou art careful and troubled about many
things; but one thing is needful.

But we will give ourselves continually to
prayer, and to the ministry of the word.

Watch ye, therefore, and pray always, that ye
may be accounted worthy to escape all these
things that shall come to pass.

Love the Lord all thy life, and call upon Him
for thy salvation.

Humble thy soul greatly; for the vengeance of
the ungodly is fire and worms.

A man can receive nothing except it be given
him.

If He prayed who was without sin, how much more becometh it a sinner to pray? (S. Cyprian)

God hears the heart, not the voice: we do more by groans than words. (S. Aug.)

Christ groaned for this reason, to set us an example of groaning. (Arnob.)

God needeth not that we should be suppliants, nor loveth subjection; this is our own advantage, and hath an eye to our profit. (Arnob.)

Prayer ascends, mercy descends. (S. Aug.)

The grace of God is fuller than prayer: God ever granteth more than we ask.

God commandeth thee to ask, and teacheth thee how to ask, and promiseth that which thou askest, and is angry if thou askest not; and yet askest thou not?

Prayer is the breviary of faith, the interpreter of hope.

We go to God by prayers, not by steps.

Faith pours forth prayer; let it be poured forth in prayer.

Go on thus:—

> Continuing in prayer:
> always praying, and not fainting;
> in spirit and in truth.

Prayers of Intercession and Pleading

FORMS OF INTERCESSION

I

For all creatures,
men,
persons compassed
with infirmity.
Churches
Catholic,
Eastern,
Western,
British.
The episcopate,
presbytery,
clergy,
Christian people.
States
of the whole earth,
Christian,
neighboring,
our own.

Rulers,
kings,
religious kings,
our own.
Councillors,
judges,
nobles,
soldiers,
sailors,
the people,
the rising generation,
schools,
those at court,
in cities,
the country.
Those who serve
the soul;
those who serve

the body,
in food,
clothing,
health,
necessaries.
[Those who have
a claim on my
prayers,]
in nature,
by benefits,

from trust,
formerly or now,
in friendship,
in love,
in neighborhood;
from promise,
from mutual offices,
from want of leisure,
from destitution,
from extremity.

II

Thy whole creation,
our whole race,
the states of the world,
the Catholic Church,
the separate Churches,
the separate states,
our Church,
our state,
the orders in each,
the persons in the
    orders,

the world,
the inhabited earth,

the Christian religion,

our country,

the priesthood,
the person of the king, of the prince,
the city,
the parish in which I was baptized,
All-Hallows, Barking.
My two schools,
my university,
my college,

the parish committed to me, St. Giles's,
the three Churches
of Southwell,
St. Paul's,
Westminster;
the three Dioceses
of Chichester,
Ely,
Winton,
my home,
my kindred,
those who shew me pity,
those who minister to me;
my neighbors,
my friends,
those who have a claim on me.

III

The creation,   the race of man,
all in affliction and in prosperity,
in error,   and in truth,
in sin,   and in grace;
the Church ecumenical,
Eastern, Western, our own,
rulers, clergy, people.
States of the earth,
Christian, neighboring, our own,
the king, the queen, the prince,
the nobles.

Parliament, law courts, army, police.
The commons,
farmers, merchants, artisans,
down to mean workmen,
and poor.
Those who have a claim on me,
from kindred,
benefaction,
ministration of things temporal,
change formerly or now,
natural kindness,
Christian love,
neighborhood,
promise on my part,
their own desire,
their lack of leisure,
sympathy for their extreme misery;
any good work,
any noble action,
any scandal from me,
having none to pray for them.

IV

World,	earth inhabited.
Church,	kingdom,
throne,	altar.
Council chamber,	law courts,
schools,	work places.

Infants,   boys,
the grown,   youths,
men,   elderly,
aged,   decrepit.

The possessed,   weak-hearted,
sick,   prisoners,
orphans,   widows,
foreigners,
travelers,   voyagers,
with child,   who give suck,
in bitter bondage,   in desolateness,
overladen.

AN ACT OF INTERCESSION

[Let us pray] for the Catholic Church;
for the Churches throughout the whole world;
      that is, for their verity, unity, and stability;
            that in all charity may flourish,
               and truth be a living principle.
                  For our Church;
      that what is wanting in it may be supplied;
            what is unsound, corrected;
      that all heresies, schisms, scandals,
               as well public as private,
                  may be removed.
            Correct the wandering,
               convert the unbelieving,

increase the faith of the Church,
destroy heresies,
expose the crafty enemies,
bruise the violent.
[Pray we] for the clergy;
that they may rightly divide,
that they may rightly walk;
that while they teach others, themselves
may learn.
For the people;
that they seek not to be wise above measure;
but may be persuaded by reason,
and yield to the authority of superiors.
For governments;
their stability and peace.
For our kingdom, incorporation, city;
that they may fare well and prosperously,
and be freed from all danger and inconvenience.
For the king:
help him now, O Lord,
O Lord, send him now prosperity;
crown him with the array of truth and glory:
speak good things to his heart
for Thy Church and people.
For the prudence of his counsellors;
the equity and integrity of the judges;
the courage of the army;
the temperance of the people,
and their godly simplicity.
For the rising generation,

whether in universities,
or in schools;
that as they increase in age,
they may also increase in wisdom and in favor
with God and man.
For them that shew themselves benevolent,
whether to the Church,
or to the poor and needy;
reward Thou them sevenfold into their bosom;
let their souls dwell at ease,
and their seed inherit the earth.
Blessed is he that considereth the
needy.

That it may please Thee to reward all
our benefactors
with eternal blessings;
for the benefits they have bestowed on
us upon earth,
let them obtain everlasting rewards in heaven.
That it may please Thee to behold and to relieve
the miseries of the poor and the captives.
That it may please Thee of Thy merciful
compassion
to restore the frail lapses of the flesh,
and to strengthen them that are falling.
That it may please Thee graciously to accept
our reasonable service.
That it may please Thee to raise our minds
to heavenly desires.

That it may please Thee to regard us
with the eyes of Thy compassion.
That it may please Thee to preserve the souls
of us and ours
from everlasting damnation.
That it may please Thee to grant unto me,
with those for whom I have prayed,
or for whom I am in any way bound to pray,
and with all the people of God,
an entrance into Thy kingdom;
there to behold Thy Presence in righteousness,
and to be satisfied with glory.
We beseech Thee to hear us, good Lord!

SUBJECTS FOR MEDITATION
BEFORE INTERCESSION

Thanks be to God for His unspeakable gift.

The Apostle meaneth by the unspeakable gift of God, the mutual offices, and prayers, and thanksgivings of many for him.

Moreover, as for me, God forbid that I should sin against the Lord in ceasing to pray for you.

In this life we know that we can be assisted by prayers: but when we shall have come before the tribunal of Christ, neither Job, nor Daniel, nor Noah, can intercede for us, but each carrieth his own load.

The Spirit itself maketh intercession for us with groanings which cannot be uttered.

Can thine or my groanings be called unutterable, when there are often none, when they are often cold? But because there is no day, no moment, in which the saints supplicate not God, one more, one less, fervently, and all make One Dove; hence the unutterable groanings, namely, the groanings of each for all, which profit all them who are in the body of the Church.

He who prays for others, labors for himself.

If thou prayest for thyself alone, thou alone wilt pray for thyself.

If thou prayest for all, all will pray for thee.

AN ACT OF PLEADING

Remember what my substance is,
  dust and ashes,
  grass and a flower,
  flesh and a wind that passeth away,
  corruption and the worm,
 as a stranger and sojourner upon earth,
  inhabiting a house of clay,
  whose days are few and evil,
  today and not tomorrow, (Prov. xxvii. 1)
  at morning and not till evening,
          (Isa. xxxviii. 13)
  now and not presently,

in a body of death,
in a world of corruption,
that lieth in wickedness.
Remember this. (Ps. lxxiv. 18)

AN ACT OF PLEADING

I. AS RESPECTS GOD.

1. *From the nature of God.*

Because the Lord is gracious and merciful,
long-suffering and of great goodness;
He will not always be chiding,
neither keepeth He His anger forever;
He hath not dealt with us after our sins,
neither rewarded us according to our
wickednesses;
for as the heaven is high above the earth,
so great is His mercy toward them that fear Him;
as far as the east is from the west,
so far hath He removed our sins from us;
even as a father pitieth his children,
even so is the Lord merciful unto them
that fear Him;
because He is long-suffering, and pitiful,
and of great mercy to all that call upon Him;
the Lord is loving unto every man,
and His mercies are over all His works;
He delighteth in mercy

He is the Father of mercies;
He is Mercy;
because His nature is to shew mercy;
and punishment is His strange and
            unaccustomed act.

2. *The Name of God.*

Let the power of my Lord be great, according as
    Thou has spoken, saying, The Lord is long-
    suffering and of great mercy, forgiving in-
    iquity and transgression.

3. *The Name of Father.*

I ascend unto my Father, and your Father.
The Father of the prodigal son.
And what wilt Thou do with Thy great name?

4. *The Name of Christ.*

The Typical Lamb. Behold! the Lamb of God!
The Redeemer. I know that my Redeemer liveth.
The Saviour. We know that this is indeed the
    Saviour.
The Mediator. There is one Mediator between
    God and man.
The Advocate. We have an Advocate with the
    Father.

The Intercessor. [He ever liveth to make intercession.]
The High Priest. [We have a great High Priest.]

5. *The Name of the Holy Ghost.*

The typical Dove. I saw the Spirit of God de-
scending like a dove.
The Unction, or Anointing. The same anointing
teacheth you of all things.
The Comforter. If I go not away, the Comforter
will not come.

6. *The promises of God.*

Remember Thy word unto Thy servant,
wherein Thou hast caused me to put my trust;
which God, that cannot lie, promised,
and confirmed by an oath;
which our unbelief shall not make of none effect;
if we believe not, yet He abideth faithful;
He cannot deny Himself.

7. *The practice of God.*

Our fathers trusted in Thee; they trusted in Thee,
and Thou didst deliver them.
Call to remembrance, O Lord, Thy
tender mercies,

and Thy loving-kindnesses, which hath been ever
of old.
Lord, where are Thy old loving-kindnesses?
Look at the generations of old, and see;
did any ever trust in the Lord, and was
confounded?
did any abide in His fear, and was forsaken?

II. AS RESPECTS OURSELVES,
RELATIVELY TO GOD.

1. *As the work and creation of His hands.*

Despise not Thou the work of Thine own hands.
We are the clay, and Thou the Potter;
and we are all the works of Thine hands.
Thou hatest nothing that Thou hast made.
(Wisd. ii. 24)

2. *As the image of His countenance;*

and so not to be destroyed.
Let us make man in Our image, after Our likeness.
Who is renewed in knowledge, after the
image of Him that created him.

3. *As the price of His Blood;*

and so not to be despised.
Ye are bought with a price,

with the precious Blood of a Lamb
without blemish, and without spot.

4. *As called by His Name.*

Despise not the express image of Thyself.
We are called by Thy Name.
Thy people are called by Thy Name.
A chosen vessel to bear Thy Name.

5. *As members of the Body of Christ;*

and so not to be cut off.
Ye are the Body of Christ, and members
in particular.
Know ye not, that your bodies are the members
of Christ?
Know ye not, that your body is the Temple
of the Holy Ghost which is in you?

6. *As having a title in Christ.*

I am Thine; save me.
Behold, O Lord, I am Thy servant;
I am Thy servant, and the son of Thine
handmaid;
an unprofitable servant, yet a servant;
a lost son, yet a son;
we are all Thy people.
Carest Thou not that we perish? Yea, Thou carest.

III. AS RESPECTS OURSELVES, RELATIVELY TO OUR NATURE.

1. *Our weakness.*

Have mercy upon me, O Lord, for I am weak.
Remember what my substance is.
He remembered that they were but flesh;
a wind that passeth away, and cometh not again.
For He knoweth our frame.
He remembereth that we are dust.
The days of man are but as grass;
for he flourisheth as a flower of the field.
For as soon as the wind goeth over it, it is gone;
and the place thereof shall know it no more.

2. *The misery of our condition.*

We are come to great misery.
He looked upon them when they were in trouble;
and heard their prayer.

IV. AS RESPECTS OURSELVES, RELATIVELY TO OUR DUE OBEDIENCE.

1. *Because we repent.*

A broken and a contrite heart, O God Thou wilt
not despise.
For I will confess my wickedness;
and be sorry for my sin.

2. *Because we pray.*

For I will call daily upon Thee.
How long wilt Thou be angry with Thy
people that prayeth?
I forgave thee all that debt, because thou
desiredst Me.

3. *Because we forgive.*

Forgive, and ye shall be forgiven.
When ye come to pray, forgive,
if ye have aught against anyone,
that your Father which is in heaven may also
forgive you.
But if ye forgive not men their trespasses,
neither will your Father forgive your trespasses.

4. *Because we purpose for the future.*

My soul breaketh out for the very fervent desire
that it hath alway unto Thy judgments.
My hands also will I lift up unto Thy
commandments which I have loved.
I have sworn, and am stedfastly purposed
to keep Thy righteous judgments.
Thy servants, who desire to fear Thy Name.
That servant, which prepared not himself,
neither did according to his Lord's will,
shall be beaten with many stripes.

V. AS RESPECTS THE EVIL WHICH WOULD ARISE FROM OUR DESTRUCTION.

1. *It will bring no advantage.*

What profit is there in my blood,
     when I go down to the pit?
Shall the dust praise Thee?
     or shall it declare Thy truth?
For in death no man remembereth Thee;
     and who will give Thee thanks in the pit?
Dost Thou shew wonders among the dead?
or shall the dead rise up again, and praise Thee?
Shall Thy loving-kindness be shewed in the grave,
     and Thy faithfulness in destruction?
Shall Thy wondrous works be known in the dark,
     and Thy righteousness in the land where all
          things are forgotten?
For the grave cannot praise Thee; death cannot
          celebrate Thee;
they that go down into the pit cannot hope for
          Thy truth.
The living, the living, he shall praise Thee.

2. *Our creation will have been in vain.*

Hast Thou made all men for nought?
Enter not into judgment with Thy servant;
for in Thy sight shall no man living be justified.
If Thou, Lord, wilt be extreme to mark what is
          done amiss,

O Lord, who may abide it?
If He will contend with him,
he cannot answer Him one of a thousand.

3. *The enemies of God will triumph.*

Give not Thine Heritage to reproach,
that the heathen should bear rule over it;
wherefore should they say among the people,
Where is their God?
Remember this, O Lord, how the enemy hath
rebuked,
and how the foolish people have blasphemed
Thy Name.
The presumption of them that hate Thee
increaseth ever more and more.
Wherefore should the Egyptians speak and say,
For mischief did he bring them out,
to slay them in the mountains, and to consume
them from the face of the earth?
The Canaanites shall say,
He was not able to bring them into the
land which He sware;
therefore He slew them in the wilderness.

VI. AS RESPECTS THE GOOD WHICH WILL ARISE FROM OUR SALVATION.

1. *The glory of God's Name.*

Deliver us, O Lord, for the glory of Thy Name:

so we that are Thy people, and the sheep of Thy
pasture,
shall give Thee thanks forever:
and will alway be shewing forth Thy praise
from generation to generation.

2. *The conversion of others.*

Then shall I teach Thy ways unto the wicked;
and sinners shall be converted unto Thee.

3. *Example.*

For this cause I obtained mercy,
that in me first Jesus Christ might shew forth
all long-suffering,
for a pattern to them which should hereafter
believe in Him
to life everlasting.

4. *The sake of God Himself.*

I, even I, am He that blotteth out thy
trangressions for Mine own sake.
O Lord, hearken and do;
defer not for Thine own sake.
[For His sake] whom God hath set forth to be
a propitiation.
Look upon the face of Thine Anointed.
Turn not away the presence of Thine Anointed.

5. *The descent of the Saviour.*

Have mercy on me, O Lord, Thou Son of David;
David said unto Shimei, Thou shalt not die;
and the king sware unto him.

6. *The office of the Saviour.*

The Spirit of the Lord God is upon Me,
because He hath anointed Me;
He hath sent Me to preach the Gospel
unto the poor,
to bind up the broken-hearted.
I came to call sinners.
God sent His Son, that the world through Him
should be saved.

AN ACT OF PLEADING

The triumph of mercy,
Thy Name's sake,
the glory of Thy name,
the truth of Thy Promise,
intervention of Thine Oath,
comfort of Love,
bowels of mercies,
Thy mercy which is manifold,
great, (Ps. li. 1)
ancient, (Ps. xxv. 6)
plenteous, (Ps. cxxx. 7)

  everlasting, (Ps. cxxxvi.)

  exceeding, (Eph. ii. 4)

  marvelous, (Ps. cxvii. 8)

 the riches of Thy mercy, (Eph. i. 7)

 its abundance, (Eph. i. 8)

 its excess, (1 Tim. i. 14)

 its superabundance, (Rom. v. 20)

  its exceeding riches, (Eph. ii. 7)

 its victory over all Thy works, (Ps. cxlv. 9)

  over justice, (James ii. 13)

 the satisfaction and merits of Christ,

 the consolation of the Holy Ghost.

Thy mercy

 by which it is that we are not consumed,

           (Lam. iii. 22)

 that preventeth, (Ps. lxxix. 8)

 followeth, (Ps. xxiii. 6)

 surroundeth, (Ps. xxxii, 10)

 forgiveth, (Ps. ciii. 3)

 crowneth, (Ps. ciii. 4)

 hath length, breadth, depth, height,

           (Eph. iii. 18)

 is from everlasting, (Ps. xxv. 6)

 to everlasting, (Ps. lxxxix. 2)

 reacheth to heaven, (Ps. cviii. 4)

 reacheth to hell, (Ps. lxxxvi. 13)

 is over all, (Rom. ii. 32)

 is tender, (Luke i. 78)

 sweet, (Ps. lxix. 16; cxxix. 21)

 better than life, (Ps. lxiii. 3)

as is Thy Majesty, (Eccles. ii. 18)
pardoning until seventy times seven,

(Matt. xviii. 12)

hating nothing that it hath made,
neglecting neither the young ravens,

(Matt. vi. 26)

  nor the sparrow,
willing that all should be saved, (1 Tim. ii. 4)
willing not that any should perish,

(2 Pet. iii. 9)

bringing back the lost sheep on the shoulder,

(Luke xv. 5)

sweeping the house for the lost drachma,

(Luke xv. 6)

forgiving the ten thousand talents,

(Matt. xviii. 27)

binding up the wounds of the half dead,

(Luke x. 34)

joyfully meeting the prodigal son,

(Luke xv. 20)

that freed the fugitive Jonah,
received the denying Peter,
did not reject the incredulous Thomas,
converted the blaspheming Saul,
liberated the woman taken in adultery,
received Mary Magdalene,
opened paradise to the thief,
standeth at the door and knocketh,
the Lord Himself entreating His own servants,

(2 Cor. v. 20)

whose place is the throne of grace,
    the mercy seat,
whose time is the Day of Salvation,
    I have deferred repentance,
      and Thou hast prolonged patience by mercy,
O Thou Fountain inexhaustible!

Prayers of Thanksgiving

SUBJECTS FOR MEDITATION
BEFORE THANKSGIVING

Praise is not comely in the mouth of fools,
    it is good before Thy saints.

All Thy works praise Thee, O Lord, and Thy
saints give thanks unto Thee.

Blessed is the people that know the joyful
sound.

All sacrifice is little in comparison with thanksgiving.

We may speak much, and yet come short.
                    (Eccles. xliii. 27)

Woe to them that are silent concerning Thee,
O Lord: for even they that speak are dumb.
                    (S. Aug. Conf. I)

He attaineth not to Thy works, but keepeth
more silence; and it seemeth to proceed from the
mouth of sucklings.

For as it was your mind to go astray from
God: so, being returned, seek Him ten times
more. (Bar. iv. 28)

That as once in sins, so now we may abound in
good works and the praises of God.

But what am I, Lord———

Make me, O Lord, to be at leisure for my penitence and Thy praises.

AN ACT OF THANKSGIVING

Let all Thy works praise Thee, O Lord,
and Thy saints give thanks unto Thee.
It is a good thing to give thanks unto the Lord,
and to sing praises unto Thy Name,
O Most High:
to tell of Thy loving-kindness
early in the morning,
and of Thy truth
in the night season.
I will exalt Thee, my God, O King,
and praise Thy Name forever and ever.
Every day will I give thanks unto Thee,
and praise Thy Name forever and ever.
Who didst call the things that were not,
as though they were;
by whom all things were made
in heaven and in earth,
visible and invisible;
who upholdest all things by the word
of Thy power;
who dost not leave Thyself without witness,
in that Thou doest good, and givest us
rain from heaven,
and fruitful seasons,
filling our hearts with joy and gladness;

in that all things continue this day
according to Thine ordinance;
for all things serve Thee;
who, having before taken counsel,
didst Thyself, with Thine own hands,
make man out of the dust of the earth,
and didst breathe into his nostrils the
breath of life;
and didst honor him with Thine image;
and didst charge Thine Angels concerning him;
and didst set him over the works of Thine hands;
and didst place him in a paradise of pleasure;
and didst not despise him, even when he despised
Thy law;
but didst open for him the door
unto repentance and life;
giving him Thy great and precious promise
concerning the Seed of the woman;
who hast instructed our race,
by that which may be known of God,
by that which is written in the
Law,
by the rite of Sacrifices,
by the oracles of the Prophets,
by the melody of the Psalms,
by the wisdom of the Proverbs,
by the experience of the Histories;
who, when the fullness of time was come,
didst send forth Thy Son,
who took the seed of Abraham,

and made Himself of no reputation,
putting on the form of a servant;
and being made of a woman,
made under the law,
by the oblation of His life accomplished
its obedience,
by the sacrifice of His death removed its curse;
redeeming our race by His passion,
quickening it by His resurrection;
leaving nothing undone, that could be done,
to make us partakers of the Divine nature;
who hath manifested in every place the savor
of His knowledge,
by the preaching of the Gospel;
bearing Himself witness
with divers signs and wonders,
by marvelous holiness of life,
by mighty power even unto shedding of blood,
by the incredible conversion of the
world to the Faith,
without assistance of authority,
without intervention of persuasion;
who hast made us children of the saints,
and heirs of the same vocation;
who hast granted to Thy Church,
that she should be the pillar and ground
of the truth;
and that the gates of hell
should not prevail against her;
who hast granted unto our Church,

that she should keep that which was
committed unto her,
and should teach us the way of peace;
who hast confirmed the throne of Thy servant,
our king;
who makest peace in our borders,
and fillest us with the flower of wheat;
who hast made fast the bars of our gates,
and hast blessed our children within us;
who hast clothed our enemies with confusion;
who givest us everlasting felicity,
and makest us glad with the joy of Thy
countenance;
who hast informed our princes,
and taught our senators wisdom;
who hast given us pastors according to
Thine heart,
that feed us with knowledge and understanding;
who hast turned our swords into ploughshares,
and our spears into pruning hooks;
who hast caused that there should be no decay,
no leading into captivity, and no complaining
in our streets;
who didst bring me forth into life,
and didst bring me on to the Laver of
Regeneration,
and renewing of the Holy Ghost;
and hast made known to me Thy ways;
and hast winked at my sins, because
I should amend: [Wisdom xi. 23]

who hast not shut me up in the hand of
mine iniquity,
waiting to shew mercy upon me;
who hast not suffered my heart to be hardened;
but hast left me compunction of soul,
remembrance of my latter end,
conscience of committed sins;
who hast opened to me a gate of hope,
while I confess and implore,
through the power of Thy mysteries
and the Keys;
who hast not cut off, like a weaver, my life,
nor made an end of me from day even to night;
nor taken me away in the midst of my days;
but hast holden my soul in life,
and hast not suffered my feet to slip.

AN ACT OF THANKSGIVING

1. *The excellence of God's majesty.*

Glorify Thou Me, O Father, with Thine own self,
with the glory which I had with Thee before
the world was.
Melchisedeck was priest of the Most High God.

2. *His exaltedness.*

He that is higher than the highest regardeth.
(Eccles. v. 8)

3. *His eternity.*

The Lord, the everlasting God. (Gen. xxi. 33)

4. *His omnipresence.*

Do I not fill heaven and earth, saith the Lord?

5. *His omniscience.*

Whither shall I go then from Thy Spirit?
or whither shall I go then from Thy Presence?
If I climb up into heaven, Thou art there;
if I go down into hell, Thou art there also.
Thou knowest all things.
For Thou only knowest the hearts of the children
of men.

6. *His omnipotence.*

With God nothing shall be impossible.
I am the Almighty God.

7. *The height of His wisdom.*

O the depth of the riches of the wisdom and
knowledge of God;
how unsearchable are His judgments!
and His ways past finding out!

8. *His unshaken truth.*

The truth of the Lord endureth forever,

heaven and earth shall pass away,
but My words shall not pass away.

9. *His exquisite justice.*

His justice endureth forever.

10. *The fountain, ocean, abyss of His mercy.*

Deep calleth unto deep.

11. *He is merciful in passing by and overlooking sin.*

I beseech you by the meekness and gentleness
of Christ.
I will not destroy it for ten's sake.
He passeth by transgressions.
The times of ignorance God winked at.

12. *He is patient, long-suffering.*

Or despisest thou the riches of His forbearance,
and long-suffering?

13. *Pitiful.*

But He was so merciful, that He forgave
their misdeeds,
and destroyed them not.

14. *He punisheth unwillingly.*

O Ephraim, what shall I do unto thee?

O Judah, what shall I do unto thee?
Yet many years didst Thou forbear them;
for Thy great mercies' sake
Thou didst not utterly consume them,
nor forsake them.
He hath not dealt with us after our sins,
neither rewardeth us according to our iniquities.
She hath received of the Lord's hand double for
all her sins.
Like as a father pitieth his own children,
even so is the Lord merciful unto them that fear
Him.

15. *Compassionate.*

He repenteth Him of the evil.

16. *His anger is soon quenched.*

He will not alway be chiding;
neither keepeth He His anger forever.

17. *He is ready to pardon.*

I forgave thee all that debt, because thou
desiredst Me.

18. *Ready to be reconciled.*

Reconciling the world unto Himself,
not imputing their trespasses unto them.

19. *Ready to be propitiated.*

Bring forth the best robe, and put it on him;
and put a ring on his hand, and shoes
on his feet: etc.
He is good and kind to the unthankful
and to the evil.

20. *Munificent.*

Giving the reward of a day for the toil of an hour.
Today shalt thou be with Me in Paradise.

Giving sight to the blind,	loosing the bound,
clothing the naked,	raising the fallen,
upholding the falling,	healing the sick,
gathering the dispersed,	feeding the living,
sustaining the faint,	quickening the dead,
casting down the proud,	setting up the humble,
redeeming the captives,	helping in time of need.

Who is like unto Thee, O Lord, among
the Gods?
glorious in holiness, fearful in praises,
doing wonders?

[Let us praise God for]
Angels, the guardians of men;
Archangels, announcing, by their illumination,
mightier events;

the voice of the Archangel:
virtues, that do wonders;
virtues being made subject unto Him.
Powers, that ward off the attacks of fiends,
    at His command;
Principalities, perfect in government;
Dominations, that bestow gifts in
    plenteousness;
Thrones, that judge at the tribunal;
        whether they be thrones, or dominions,
        or principalities, or powers,
        all things were created by Him and for
            Him.
Cherubim, glittering with knowledge;
    He placed Cherubim before paradise;
Seraphim, ardent with love;
        above it stood the Seraphim: each one had
            six wings.
The morning stars,
rulers of the world,
lovers of men,
chief ministers of the Divine will;
        [we laud God for the] perseverance of
            Angels;
        [we pray that we] going from strength
            to strength,
        may be associated with their choirs.

            [We praise Him for]
The Patriarchs and their faith,

The Prophets and their hope,
The Apostles and their labors,
The Evangelists and their truth,
The Martyrs and their blood,
The Confessors and their zeal,
The Doctors and their study,
The Asceticks and their tears,
The Virgins, flowers of purity,
        celestial gems,
        brides of the Immaculate Lamb;
The Innocents and their beauty,
        flowers of the Church,
        mirrors of virtue,
        tabernacles of the Holy Ghost.
For those, whose faith was strong, and whose
        life approved;
        in whose heart was charity,
        in whose mouth verity,
        in whose life piety.

[We praise Him] for
        light,
        the waters and the heaven,
        the earth and the plants,
        the luminaries,
        the fishes and the fowls,
        the wild and tame beasts,
        the rest of the Sabbath.
For the formation of man,
        after counsel held,

with His own hands,
with the breath of life,
in the image [of God],
for the dominion over the creatures,
the care of Angels,
the location in paradise,
that he was not forsaken, when he had sinned.
For the promise of the Seed of the woman,
that which may be known of God,
the works of the law written in the heart,
the oracles of the Prophets,
the music of the Psalms,
the wisdom of the Proverbs,
the experience of the Histories.
For our birth,
bringing up,
preservation,
direction,
instruction,
civilized state,
religion.
For redemption,
the great mystery of godliness,
His being made of no reputation,
His humiliation,
taking the seed of Abraham,
union to it,
oblation of life,
sacrifice of death.

For all the good that He did therein,
    all the evil He suffered,
    in His passage from the cradle to the cross.
For the whole design of grace,
    the Holy Incarnation,
    the poverty of His nativity,
    His lying in the manger,
    His circumcision, subjecting Him to the
      law,
    the first fruits of His Blood,
    the precious name, JESUS,
    His Epiphany to sinners of the Gentiles,
    His presentation in the Temple,
    His flight into Egypt,
    His desire of hearing,
    His eagerness to inquire,
    His humility in obeying His parents.
For His Holy Baptism,
    the appearance therein of the Trinity,
    His fasting,
    His temptation,
    His want, in that He had not where to lay
      His head,
    the hunger and thirst that He endured,
    the cold and heat,
    the weariness, while He went about doing
      good,
    His watchings,   }
    His continuance all night, }in prayer.

For His meek conversation,
>who endured such contradiction of
>>sinners;
when He was hurried to the precipice
>for a good word;
when about to be stoned
>for a good work.
[We bless Thee, O Saviour,]
>who didst endure to be insulted of men,
>to be called a Samaritan, a glutton,
>a demoniac, a deceiver,
>and wast content that Barabbas should be
>>preferred to Thee;
for Thy sermons, homilies,
>conversations, discourses,
>intercessions, prayers,
>examples,
>signs,
>mysteries,
and for the power of the Keys;
for the blessings conveyed by all the grace and
loving-kindness of Thy miracles;
for the parables of
>the Two Debtors,
>the Good Samaritan,
>the Publican and the Pharisee,
>the Servant that owned ten thousand
>>talents,
>the Good Shepherd,

the Prodigal Son,
the Called at the Eleventh Hour.

For Thy Sayings:

For God sent not His Son into the world
to condemn the world; but that the
world through Him might be saved.

I came not to judge the world, but to save
the world.

I came not to call the righteous, but
sinners to repentance.

The Son of Man is not come to destroy
men's lives, but to save them.

The Son of Man is come to seek and to
save that which was lost;

And to give His life a ransom for many.

Come unto Me, all ye that labor and are
heavy laden,
and I will give you rest.

Him that cometh unto Me I will in no
wise cast out.

Father, forgive them; for they know not
what they do.

Today shalt thou be with Me in paradise.

I will give unto this last, even as unto thee.

For the instances of Thy mercy:

The Syrophoenician or Canaanitish
woman;

the woman of Samaria;

the woman with an issue of blood;

the woman taken in adultery;

S. Mary Magdalene;
Zacchaeus;
the thief;
S. Peter;
S. Thomas;
S. Paul;
Nicodemus.

THIS MAN RECEIVETH SINNERS.

[For Thy long-suffering when]
they contradicted Thee;
drew Thee to the brow of the hill;
twice would have stoned Thee;
    and that for a good work;
blasphemed Thee;
preferred Barabbas unto Thee;
gave Thee up unto the Gentiles to crucify
    Thee.
For the death of CHRIST;
His obedience unto the death of the cross.
His straitening [till it was accomplished].
For all that He suffered,
in Gethsemane,
in Gabbatha,
in Calvary.
For the pain,
the shame,
the curse, of the cross.
That He deigned to be betrayed,
and that by His own disciple;

that He deigned to be sold,
      and that for thirty pieces of silver;
   to be troubled in His mind,
   to be weary,
   to fear,
   to be exceeding sorrowful, even unto
      death,
   to be in an agony,
   with strong crying,
   and tears,
   to sweat great drops of blood,
   even to the bedewing of the ground:
   Gethsemane,
   that His disciples should slumber,
   one of them betray Him with a kiss,
   the rest should be offended because of
      Him,
   and flee;
   to be left alone,
   and denied by Peter,
   and that with an oath,
   and a curse;
   to be subjected to the powers of darkness,
   to be laid hands on,
   taken as a thief,
   bound,
   carried away,
   hurried to Annas,
   Caiaphas,
   Pilate,

    Herod,
    Pilate the second time,
    the Praetorium,
    Gabbatha,
    the cross.
Thou that wast silent before the judge,
      restrain my tongue;
Thou that didst deign to be bound,
      restrain my hands.
[We praise Thee]
    in that Thou wast struck with the palm of
      the hand before Annas,
    accused before Caiaphas,
    attacked by false witnesses,
    condemned for blasphemy,
    derided manifold,
    mocked by the servants,
    buffeted,
    struck with the palm of the hand,
    wast blinded,
    stricken,
    spit upon,
    reviled,
    blasphemed:
    Thy head was crowned with thorns,
      and struck with the reed,
    Thine eyes dim with tears,
    Thine ears filled with reviling,
    Thy mouth given to drink of gall and
      vinegar,

Thy face marred with spitting,
Thy back ploughed with the scourge,
Thy neck bent down with the cross,
Thy hands extended,
Thy knees bent as in prayer,
Thy feet pierced with nails,
Thy heart oppressed with grief,
Thy side pierced with the lance;
Thy Blood flowing in all sides plenteously
    around Thee;
Thy Soul in bitterness,
    and Thy cry of agony,
      "Eli, Eli!"
[We praise Him that
He deigned] to be accused before Pilate of
  sedition,
    to be denied by His own,
    rejected for Barabbas.
[He deigned] to be sent bound to Herod,
    to be clothed with a white robe,
    to be mocked.
[He deigned] to be sent back to Pilate,
    to be clamored against for death,
    to be condemned to a shameful death,
    to be given up to the will of the soldiers,
    to be arrayed in purple,
    to be crowned with thorns,
    to be mocked with a reed for a sceptre,
    to be bowed the knee to,
    to be called King in derision,

  to be spit upon,
  to be smitten on the head with the reed,
  to be stripped of the purple.
[He deigned] to be bound to a column in the
 judgment hall,
  to be beaten with rods,
  to be scourged,
  to be baptized with a baptism of blood,
  to suffer bruises and wounds,
  to be demanded with clamor for
   crucifixion,
  to be exhibited as a spectacle of woe,
    BEHOLD THE MAN!
  to be cried out against the more
  vehemently,
  to be condemned to the cross.
[He deigned] to be laden with the cross,
  led to the place of punishment,
  to sink under the cross,
  to have myrrh given Him to drink,
  to endure the shame of being stripped,
  the agony of being extended on the cross,
  to be pierced with nails,
  to have hands and feet riven,
  to be crucified between two thieves,
  to be reckoned among the transgressors,
  to be reviled by the passers-by,
  to be blasphemed by the very thieves, on
  Golgotha.
[He deigned] to be forsaken of God,

to be mocked in His cry to God,
to thirst,
to have vinegar given Him to drink,
to bow the head,
give up the Ghost,
that His side should be pierced with the
    spear,
to be blasphemed after death,
to be called a deceiver,
to suffer unknown sufferings.
By Thy woes, which I unworthy here
  commemorate,
      preserve my soul from the woes of hell!

The Seven Last Words.

1. FATHER, FORGIVE THEM; FOR THEY
   KNOW NOT WHAT THEY DO.
2. WOMAN, BEHOLD THY SON!
3. TODAY, SHALT THOU BE WITH ME IN
   PARADISE.
4. ELI, ELI.
5. I THIRST.
6. IT IS FINISHED.
7. FATHER, INTO THY HANDS, I COMMEND
   MY SPIRIT.

Thou, Who didst deign
that Thy glorious head should be wounded,
  forgive thereby whatever, by the senses
      of my head, I have sinned.

That Thy holy hands should be pierced,
forgive thereby, whatever I have done amiss
by unlawful touch,
or illicit operation.
That Thy precious side should be
opened,
forgive thereby whatever I have
offended
by lawless thoughts,
in the ardor of passion.
That Thy blessed feet should be riven,
forgive thereby whatever I have done
by the means of feet swift to evil.
That Thy whole Body should be
distended,
forgive thereby whatever iniquity I have
committed
by the intervention of all my members.

And I, too, O Lord, am wounded in soul;
behold the multitude,
the length, the breadth, the depth,
of my wounds;
and by Thine, heal mine.

Thy precious death,
Thy riven side,
the streams of Water and Blood,
the begging of Thy Body,
Thy taking down from the cross,

Thy burial in the garden of another,
Thy three days' sepulture:
   By all these things I remind and beseech
      Thee;
I pray Thee that Thou wouldest deign to lay all
      these things before Thy Father,
         pleading them for my sake;
      all the sufferings which Thou barest;
   the love above all by which Thou barest.

[We praise Him for]
   His Transfiguration;
His triumph over principalities, and leading
         them captive,
      and over the powers of darkness in Himself;
   His mighty Resurrection;
   His appearance to S. Mary Magdalene,
   to the women,
   to S. Peter,
   to the two that went to Emmaus,
   to the Ten without S. Thomas,
   to the Eleven,
   at the sea of Tiberias,
   to S. James,
   to the Five Hundred,
   in Bethany.
   His glorious Ascension,
   session at the right hand,
   distribution of gifts,

continual pleading for us,
return to judgment.

> For the Holy Ghost,
> Come, Holy Ghost, our souls inspire,
> And lighten with celestial fire;
> Thou the Anointing Spirit art,
> Who dost Thy sevenfold gifts impart.

In the Old Testament,
> Thy moving upon the face of the
> waters,
> Thy emission into all things living,
> Thy inspiration of man,
> of Bezaleel,
> of the Seventy Elders,
> Thy descent upon the Prophets.

Thy visible Advent:
As a shadow;
The coming upon and overshadowing
at the Incarnation of Christ.

As a Dove:
Thy coming in the shape of a dove upon Christ
in Baptism.

> As fiery tongues:
> after the Ascension:
Thy invisible Advent:
> on the Apostles gathered together in
> prayer,
> on Cornelius,
> on the twelve Ephesians.

Thy often visitations thenceforth:
  In calling;
  calling away from sin;
  calling out of the world,
     recalling from backsliding;
  In our calling on Thee;
  in Thy pleading for us;
Thy distribution of graces, ministrations,
    operations.
The graces of the Spirit; works, fruits.
The compunction caused by Thy reproval,
  the unction of Thy teaching,
  and calling to memory,
  Thy shedding forth of love,
  Thy helping our infirmities, in praying,
  Thy witnessing our adoption,
  Thy sealing in Thy mysteries,
  the Earnest of our inheritance.
    Thy visiting us,—to visit the heart,
    dwelling in us,
    purifying us,
    shining on us,—illumination,
    strengthening us,
    adorning us,
    leading us to perfection;
  the Guide unto truth,
    the suppliance of strength.

AN ACT OF THANKSGIVING

It would rather behove me, O Lord,
  a sinner, and impenitent, and so, wholly
          unworthy,
    to lie prostrate before Thee,
  and with tears and groanings to entreat the
          pardon of my sins,
    than to praise Thee with polluted mouth;
  yet trusting in Thine innate goodness, I will
          adore Thee;
    oh, receive Thou the praises that it is in my
          heart to sing.
  I praise Thee, I bless Thee, I worship Thee,
          I glorify Thee;
    Thou art worthy, O Lord, to receive the
          praises and the thanks,
      Whom I, a sinner, am unworthy to invoke,
    and to name, and even to conceive in my
          heart.
Blessed art Thou, O Lord,
  Who hast created and brought me forth into
          this life,
    and hast ordered that I should be a living
          soul and not senseless matter:
  a man, not a brute; civilized, not barbarous;
  free, not a slave; legitimate, not spurious;
  of good parentage; not sprung from vile
          extraction, and as vile myself;

endued with sense, not an idiot;
sound in senses, not blind nor deaf;
sound in limbs, not halt nor maimed;
educated, not exposed;
brought up to literature, not to a mechanical
          trade;
a Christian, not a pagan;
preserved from dangers and infamy, not
          overwhelmed thereby;
in the days of peace, not tossed in tempestuous
          struggles;
of competent fortune, so that I need neither to
          flatter nor to borrow;
set free from many sins;
endued with the gifts of grace, in redemption
          and calling;
with the gifts of nature and fortune.
Who according to Thy great mercy, hast
     begotten us again unto a lively hope,
  by the resurrection of Jesus Christ:
     unto an inheritance incorruptible and
       undefiled, and that fadeth not away;
       reserved in heaven for us:
Who hast blessed me with all spiritual blessings
          in heavenly things in Christ;
Who comfortest me in all my tribulation,
   that as the passions of Christ abound in me,
       so also my consolation should abound
          through Christ.
To Thee, O God of my fathers, I give thanks;

Thee I praise, who hast in some measure
endued me with wisdom and courage;
and hast shewed me that which I requested of
Thee,
and hast opened my mouth:
[and hast caused me to be] the work of Thine
hands, and the price of Thy Blood;
and the image of Thy countenance, and the
servant of Thy purchase;
and the seal of Thy Name, and the child of
Thine adoption;
and the temple of Thy Spirit, and a
member of Thy Church.

AN ACT OF THANKS

O Lord, I am less than all Thy mercies,
and all Thy truth, which Thou hast shewed
unto Thy servant;
and what can I say more unto Thee?
for Thou, Lord God, knowest Thy servant.
What is Thy servant, Lord God, and what is
my house,
that Thou shouldest look on such a dead dog
as I am?
that Thou has loved me hitherto?
what shall I render unto the Lord for all the
benefits that He hath done unto me?
what thanks can we render unto God

for all the joy wherewith we joy before
Him?
Thou who hast deigned, O Lord, in this holy
day, and at this hour,
to raise my mind to Thy praise,
and to offer Thee the glory due unto Thee,
receive, O Lord, this spiritual sacrifice from my
soul;
and receiving it to Thee unto Thy spiritual
altar,
be pleased in its stead to send me the grace
of Thy Most Holy Spirit.
Visit me in Thy goodness;
forgive me every sin, as well voluntary as
involuntary.
Deliver me from eternal punishment:
yea, and from all the miseries of this world.
Change my thoughts into piety;
sanctify my spirit, soul and body;
and give me grace to worship and to please
Thee in piety and holiness of life,
even until the very end of my days.
To Him, that is able to do exceeding abundantly
above all that we ask or think,
according to the power that worketh in us,
to Him be glory in the Church in Christ,
throughout all ages, world without end.
My soul shall be satisfied as it were with marrow
and fatness;

and my mouth shall praise Thee with joyful
lips.

AN ACT OF ADORATION

O God the Father, of heaven
who didst marvelously create the world out of
nothing,
who governest and sustainest heaven and earth
with Thy power,
who, for our sakes didst give Thine
Only-begotten to be put to death:
O God the Son, Redeemer of the world,
who didst deign to be born of the Virgin,
who didst wash us from our sins in Thy
precious Blood,
who rising from the dead didst ascend Victor
into heaven:
O God the Holy Ghost, the Comforter,
who in the form of a dove didst descend upon
Jesus,
who didst appear upon the apostles like eleven
tongues of fire,
who visited and confirmest with Thy grace
the hearts of Thy saints;
Holy, Supreme, Eternal, Blessed, and Glorious
Trinity,
ever laudable, yet ever ineffable;

Father of goodness, Son of love,
    Spirit of bounty,
whose Majesty is inscrutable,
and Power incomparable,
and Goodness inestimable,
Whose Work is life,
Whose Love is grace,
Whose Contemplation is glory;
Deity, Divinity, Unity, Trinity,
    Thee I adore, Thee I invoke, Thee with the
            whole affection of my heart,
I bless now and ever,
Thou, who art Lord of both quick and dead,
whose are we, whom this present world yet
                        retaineth in the flesh,
whose are they also, whom the life to come hath
        already received, freed from the body,
    give to the quick loving-kindness and grace;
    give to the dead rest and eternal light;
    give to Thy Church truth and peace;
    and to us sinners penitence and pardon.

A PREPARATION TO
THANKSGIVING

Be Thou exalted, Lord, in Thine own strength;
    So will we sing and praise Thy power.
All Thy works praise Thee, O Lord:
    and Thy saints give thanks unto Thee.

O Lord, open Thou my lips;
    and my mouth shall shew forth Thy praise.

DOXOLOGIES

Glory to God in the highest; on earth peace;
    good-will toward men. (Luke ii. 14)
Hosanna to the Son of David. (Matt. xxi. 9)
Hosanna; blessed is the King of Israel that cometh
    in the name of the Lord. (John xii. 13)
Holy, Holy, Holy, Lord God Almighty, which
    was, and is, and is to come. (Rev. iv. 8)

OF THE ANGELS

Worthy is the Lamb that was slain
    to receive power, and riches, and wisdom, and
    strength, and honor, and glory, and blessing.

OF ALL CREATURES

Blessing, honor, glory, and power, be unto Him
    that sitteth upon the throne, and unto the Lamb
    forever and ever.

OF THE MARTYRS

Salvation to our God which sitteth
    upon the throne, and unto the Lamb.
Amen: Blessing, and glory, and wisdom,
    and thanksgiving, and honor, and power,
    and might, be unto our God forever
    and ever.

Prayers for Holy Communion

FOR HOLY COMMUNION

O Lord,
I am not worthy, I am not fit,
that Thou shouldest come under the roof
of my soul;
for it is all desolate and ruined;
nor hast Thou in me fitting place
to lay Thy head.
But, as Thou didst vouchsafe
to lie in the cavern and manger of brute cattle,
as Thou didst not disdain
to be entertained in the house of Simon the leper,
as Thou didst not disdain
that harlot, like me, who was a sinner,
coming to Thee and touching Thee;
as Thou abhorredst not
her polluted and loathsome mouth;
nor the thief upon the cross
confessing Thee:
so me too the ruined, wretched,
and excessive sinner,
deign to receive to the touch and partaking
of the immaculate, supernatural, life-giving,
and saving mysteries
of Thy All-holy Body

and Thy precious Blood.
Listen, O Lord, our God,
from Thy holy habitation,
and from the glorious throne of Thy kingdom,
and come to sanctify us.
O Thou who sittest on high with the Father,
and art present with us here invisibly;
come Thou to sanctify the gifts which
lie before Thee,
and those in whose behalf, and by whom,
and the things for which,
they are brought near Thee.
And grant to us communion,
unto faith, without shame,
love without dissimulation,
fulfilment of Thy commandments,
alacrity for every spiritual fruit;
hindrance of all adversity,
healing of soul and body;
that we too, with all saints,
who have been well-pleasing to Thee from the
beginning,
may become partakers
of Thy incorrupt and everlasting goods,
which Thou hast prepared, O Lord, for
them that love Thee;
in whom Thou art glorified
forever and ever.
Lamb of God,
that takest away the sin of the world,

take away the sin of me,
the utter sinner.

A PREPARATION FOR HOLY
COMMUNION

[Unto a pledge of communion. (Acts ii. 42)
A memorial of the Dispensation. (Eph. iii. 2)
A showing forth of His death. (1 Cor. xi. 26)
A communion of Body and Blood. (Luke xxii. 19)
A sharing in the Spirit. (1 Cor. xii. 13)
Remission of sins. (Matt. xxvi. 28)
A riddance of things contrary. (1 Cor. v. 7)
Rest of conscience. (Matt. xi. 29)
Blotting out of debts. (Col. ii. 14)
Cleansing of stains. (Heb. ix. 14)
Healing of the soul's sicknesses. (1 Pet. ii. 24)
Renewing of the covenant. (Ps. ii. 5)
Food of spiritual life. (John vi. 27)
Increase of strengthening grace. (Heb. xiii. 9)
And of winning consolation. (Luke ii. 25)
Compunction of penitence. (2 Cor. vii. 9)
Illumination of mind. (Luke xxiv. 31)
Exercise of humility. (1 Pet. v. 5)
Seal of faith. (2 Cor. i. 22)
Fullness of wisdom. (Rom. xi. 33)
Bond of love. (John xiii. 35)
Call for a collection. (1 Cor. xvi. 1)
A means of endurance. (1 Pet. iv. 1)

Liveliness of thanksgiving. (Ps. cxvi. 12)
Confidence of prayer. (*Ibid.* 13)
Mutual indwelling. (John vi. 56)
Pledge of the resurrection. (*Ibid.* 34)
Acceptable defense in judgment. (Luke xiv. 18)
Covenant of the inheritance. (Luke xii. 20)
Figure of perfection. (John xvii. 23)]
    We then remembering, O Sovereign Lord,
       in the presence of Thy holy mysteries,
       the salutary passion of Thy Christ,
          His life-giving cross,
          most precious death,
          three days' sepulture,
         resurrection from the dead,
         ascent into heaven,
  session at the right hand of Thee, the Father,
       His fearful and glorious coming;
       we beseech Thee, O Lord,
     that we, receiving in the pure testimony
        of our conscience,
      our portion of Thy sacred things,
may be made one with the holy Body and Blood
        of Thy Christ;
    and receiving them not unworthily,
we may hold Christ indwelling in our hearts,
     and may become a temple
       of Thy Holy Spirit.
       Yea, O our God,
      nor make any of us guilty
    of Thy dreadful and heavenly mysteries,

nor infirm in soul or body
from partaking of them unworthily.
But grant us
until our last and closing breath
worthily to receive a hope of Thy holy things,
for sanctification, enlightening, strengthening,
a relief of the weight of my many sins,
a preservative against all satanic working,
a riddance and hindrance of my evil conscience,
a mortification of my passions,
an appropriation of Thy commandments,
an increase of Thy Divine grace;
and a securing of Thy kingdom.

AFTER COMMUNION

It is finished and done,
so far as in our power,
Christ our God,
the mystery of Thy dispensation.
For we have held remembrance of Thy death,
we have seen the figure of Thy resurrection,
we have been filled with Thy endless life,
we have enjoyed Thy uncloying dainties,
which graciously vouchsafe all of us,
in the world to come.
Lord, the good God,
pardon every soul,
that purifieth his heart to seek God,

the Lord God of His fathers,
though he be not cleansed
according to the purification of the sanctuary.

A EUCHARISTIC PRAYER

The things which I believe to have been done
for me,
which I call to remembrance, for which I
return thanks,
which I remember, of which I put Thee in
remembrance, which I commemorate,
which I offer, which I pray Thee to offer;
of these things make me a partaker, and apply
them to me.
By the things which Thou didst, and bearest,
Thy Oblation and Sacrifice,
Thy emptying Thyself, Thy humbling
Thyself,
Thy Incarnation, Thy Conception,
Thy Birth, Thy Circumcision, the first fruits
of Thy Blood,
Thy Baptism, Thy Fasting,
Thy Temptation, Thy Houselessness, Thy
Hunger, Thy Weariness,
Thy Thirst, Thy Sleeplessness, Thy Injuries:
Thy patience, endurance,
Thy apprehension as a thief, bonds.
By Gethsemane, Gabbatha, Golgotha,

Thy obedience unto death, Thy endurance
to the cross:
Let my prayer ascend; turn not away Thine
ear.
As Thou didst deliver our Fathers, deliver us,
O Lord!
Noah from the deluge,
Abraham from Ur of the Chaldees,
Isaac from sacrifice,
[Lot from Sodom,]
Jacob from Laban and Esau,
Joseph from the calumnies of his mistress, the
prison,
Job from the temptations,
Moses from Pharaoh, and from being stoned,
Thy people from the Red Sea, and from
Babylon,
David from Saul, Goliath, Keilah, Ahitophel,
Absalom, Doeg, Sheba,
Elias from Jezebel,
Hezekiah from Rabshakeh and the sickness,
Esther from Haman,
Joash from Athaliah,
Jeremiah from the pit,
the Three Children from the furnace,
Jonah from the belly of the whale,
the disciples from the storm,
Peter from the prison of Herod,
Paul from the shipwreck, stoning, evil beasts;
Even so deliver us, O Lord, that put our trust
in Thee.